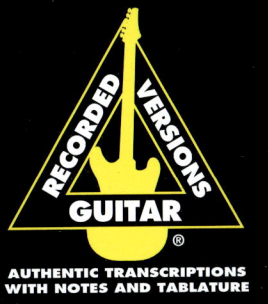

P.O.D.
THE FUNDAMENTAL ELEMENTS OF SOUTHTOWN

Page	Title
9	Greetings
11	Hollywood
18	Southtown
23	Checkin' Levels
25	Rock the Party (Off the Hook)
29	Lie Down
36	Set Your Eyes to Zion
42	Lo Siento
43	Psalm 150
45	Image
49	Shouts
50	Tribal
56	Freestyle
60	Follow Me
64	Outkast
70	Tambura

MUSIC TRANSCRIPTIONS BY PETE BILLMANN, COLIN HIGGINS AND JEFF STORY
ILLUSTRATIONS BY JEAN BASTARACHE
"BULLET THE BLUE SKY" OMITTED DUE TO COPYRIGHT RESTRICTION

ISBN 0-634-02329-2

7777 W. BLUEMOUND RD. P.O. BOX 13819 MILWAUKEE, WI 53213

For all works contained herein:
Unauthorized copying, arranging, adapting, recording or public performance is an infringement of copyright.
Infringers are liable under the law.

Visit Hal Leonard Online at
www.halleonard.com

P.
O.
D.

Photo by Rick Gould

Photo by Zach Lazarus

Photo by Rick Gould

Photo by Zach Lazarus

Photo by Zach Lazarus

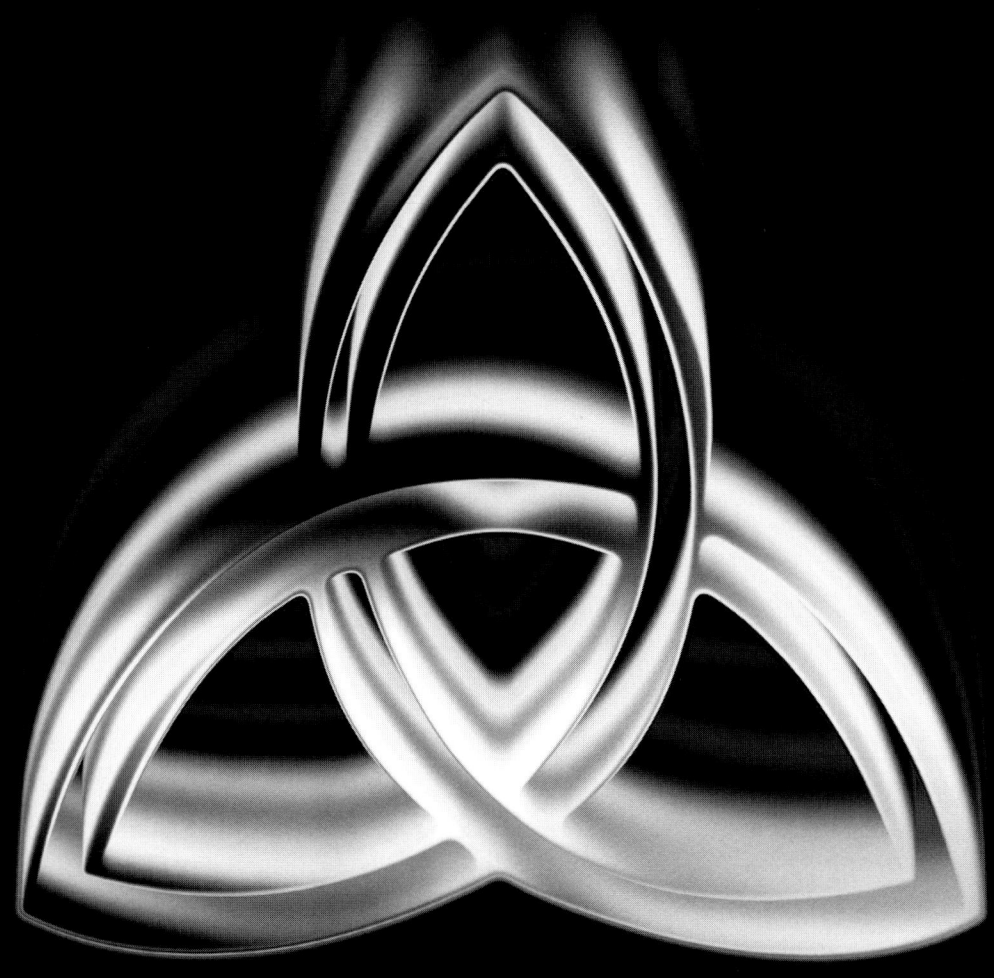

Dear Friends,

First off, I would like to take some time out to say "thank you very much" for purchasing this book of music, *The Fundamental Elements of Southtown*, which is a major piece of our hearts. I hope you enjoy playing along with us, feeling the groove that we feel each time we pick up our instruments. Have lots of fun, and enjoy yourself to the fullest!

Peace and Love

God bless,

Marcos

www.payableondeath.com

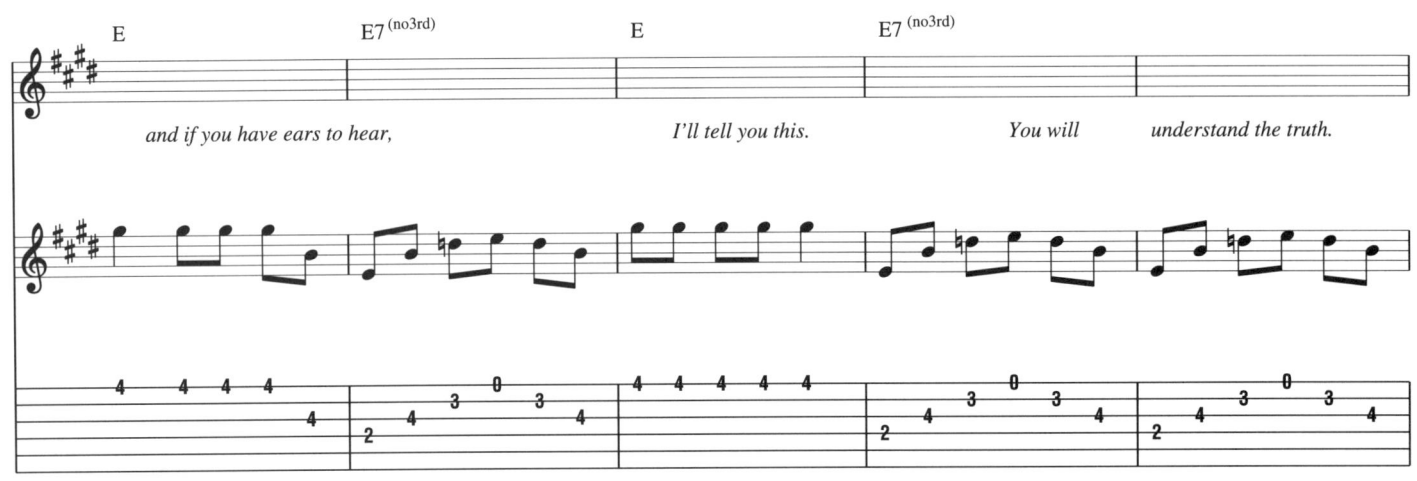

*Band only.

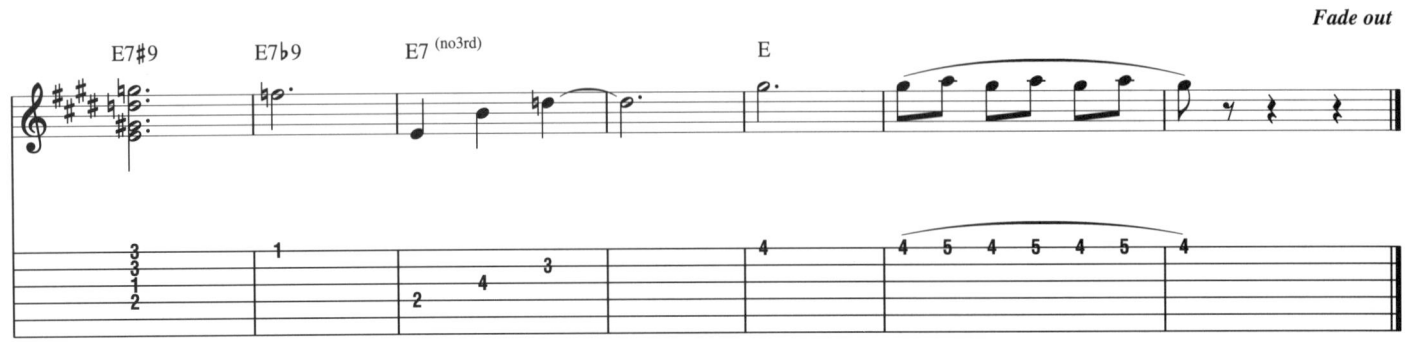

Hollywood

Words and Music by Sonny, Marcos, Traa and Wuv

Tune down 1 step:
(low to high) D–G–C–F–A–D

Intro
Moderately fast ♩ = 128

* Two gtr. arr. for one.
** Chord symbols reflect implied harmony.

Verse
Half-time feel

1st time, Gtr. 1: w/ Rhy. Fill 1

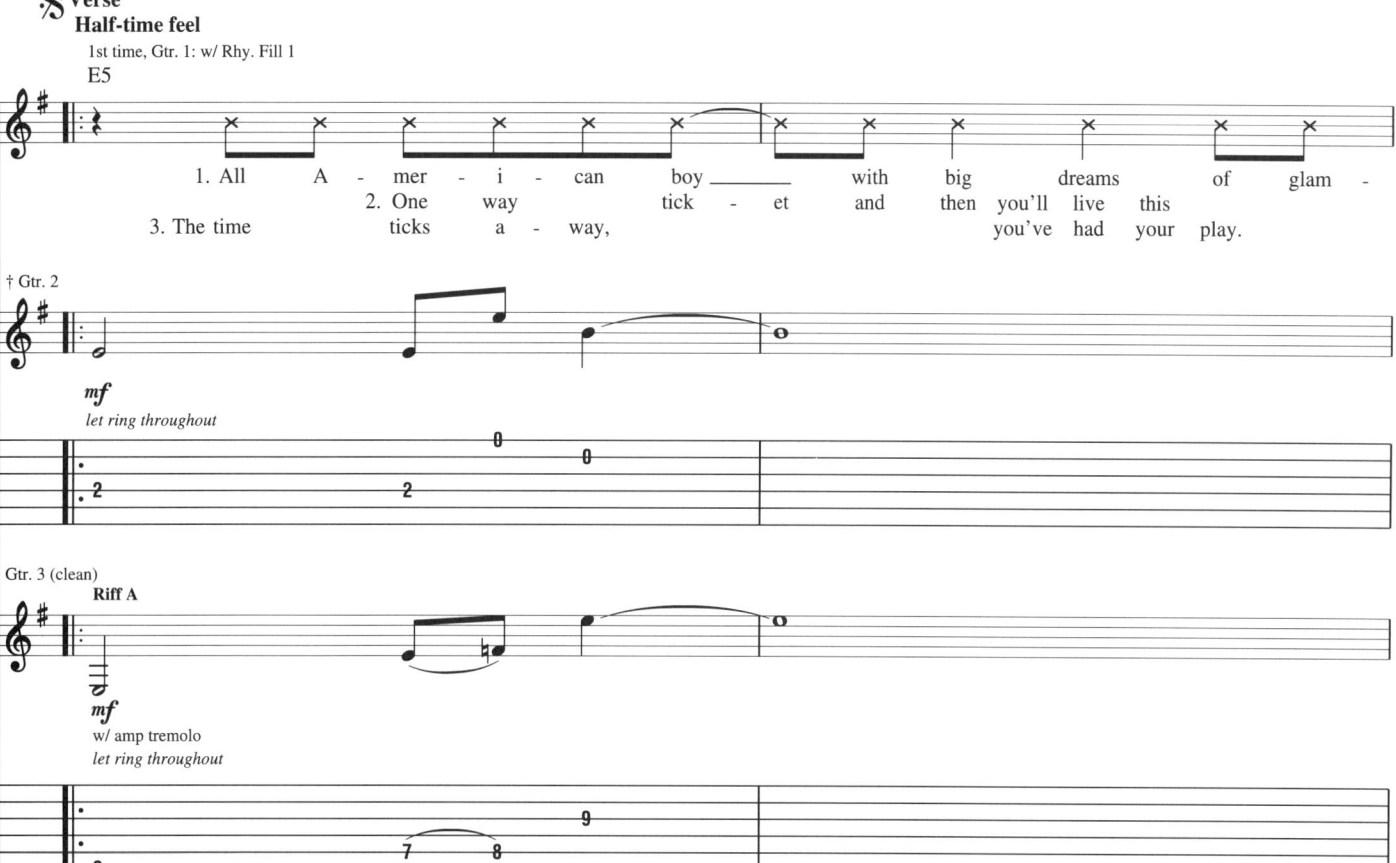

1. All A - mer - i - can boy with big dreams of glam -
2. One way tick - et and then you'll live this
3. The time ticks a - way, you've had your play.

† Banjo arr. for gtr.

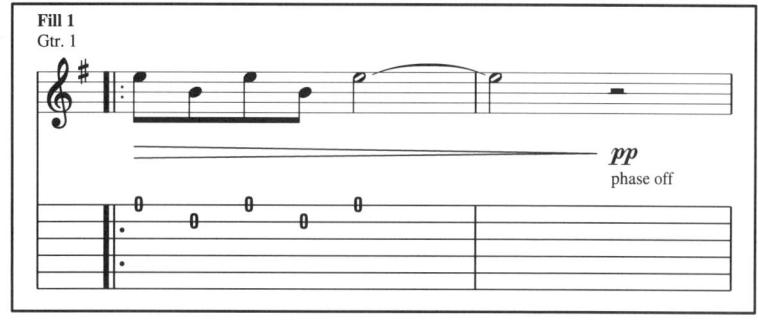

Copyright © 1999 by Souljah Music and Famous Music Corporation
International Copyright Secured   All Rights Reserved

11

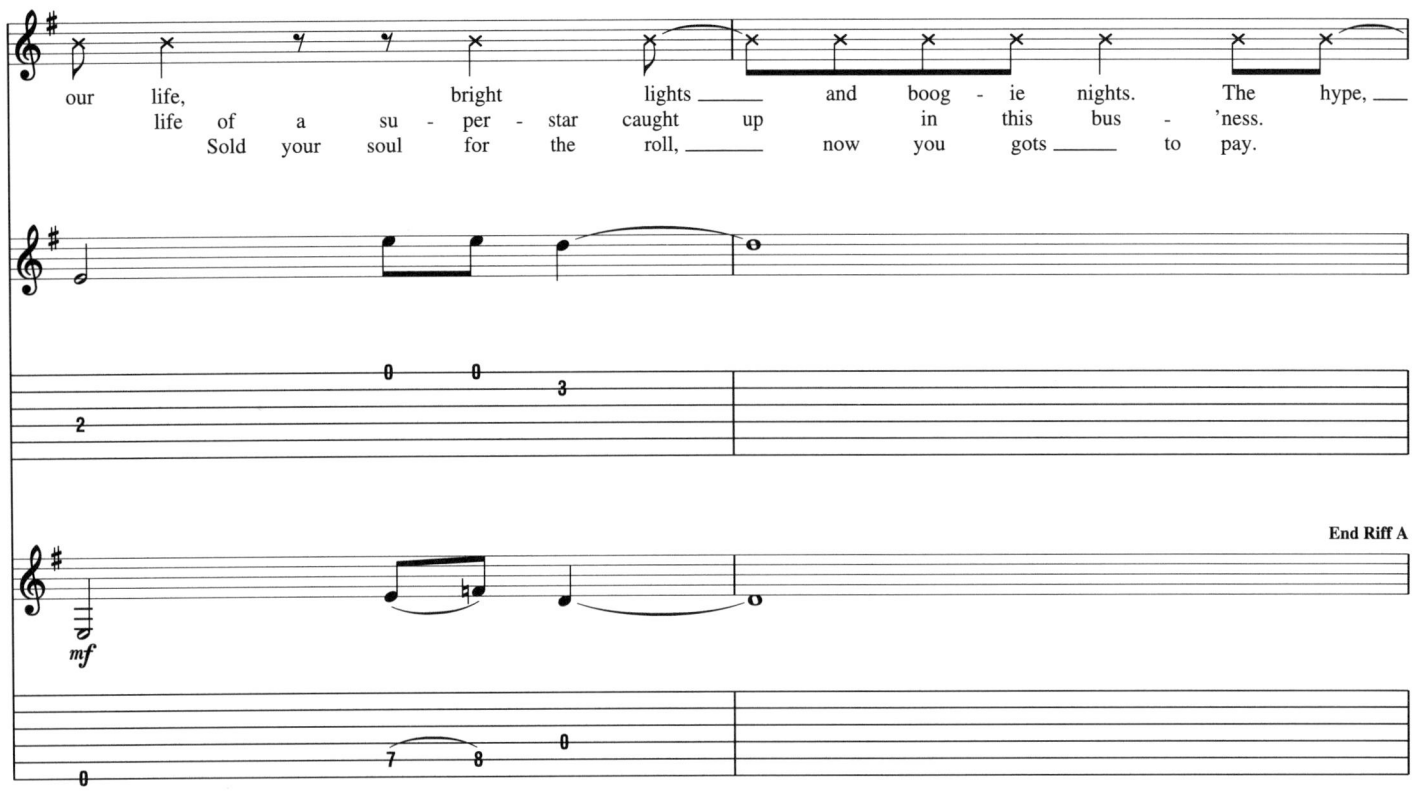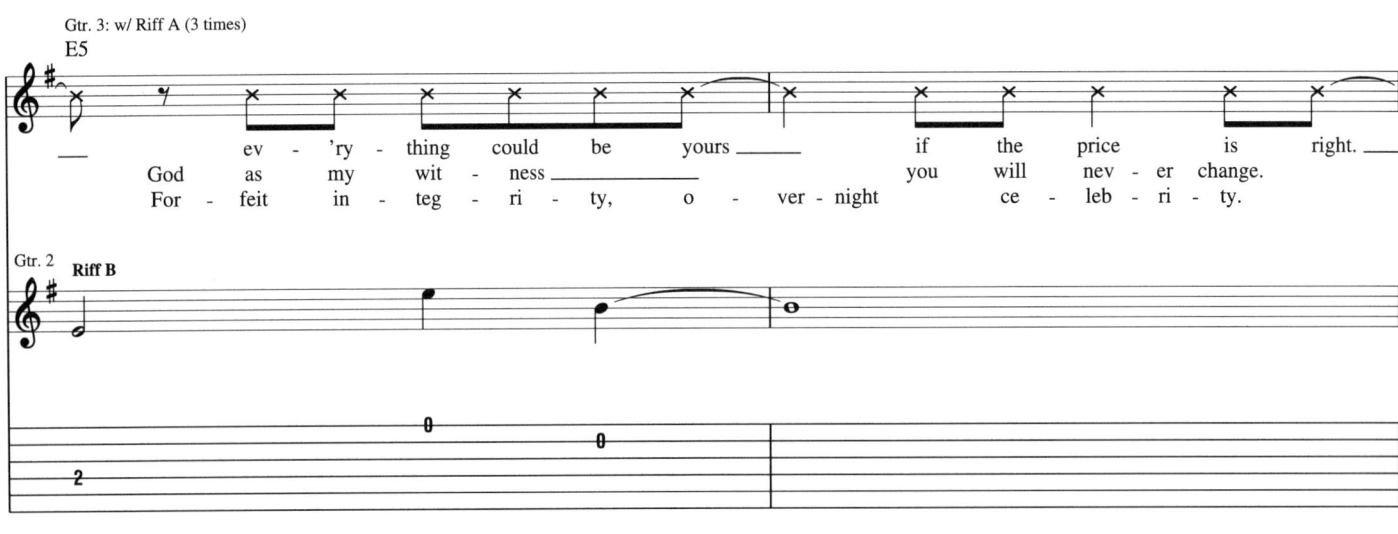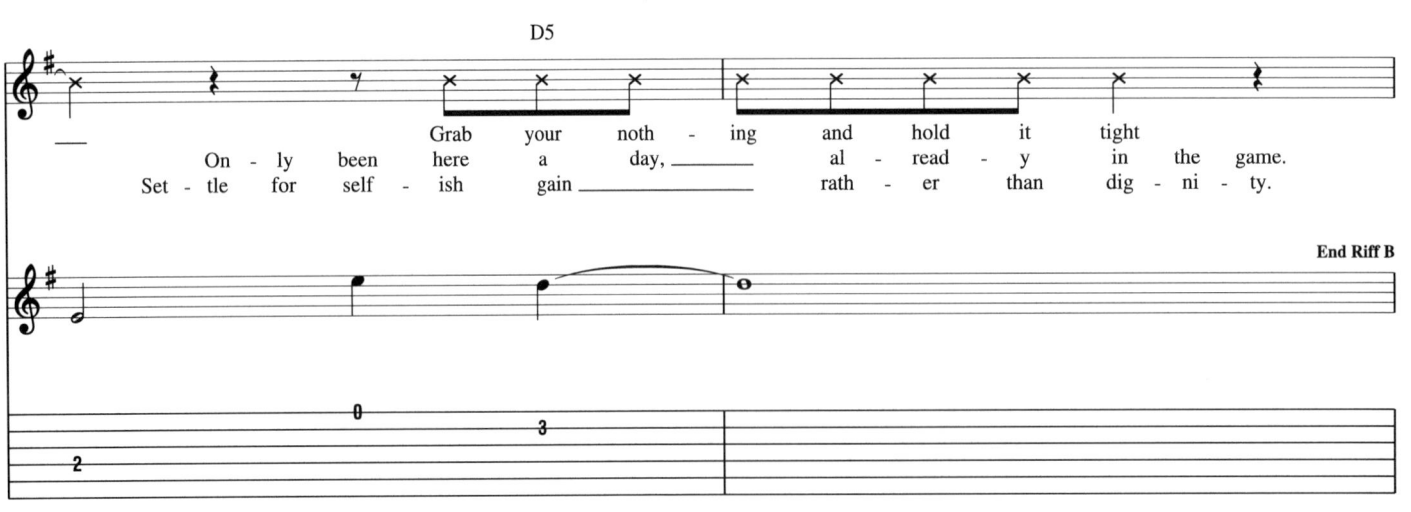

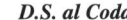

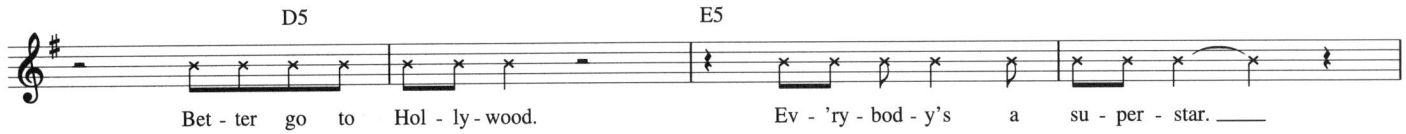
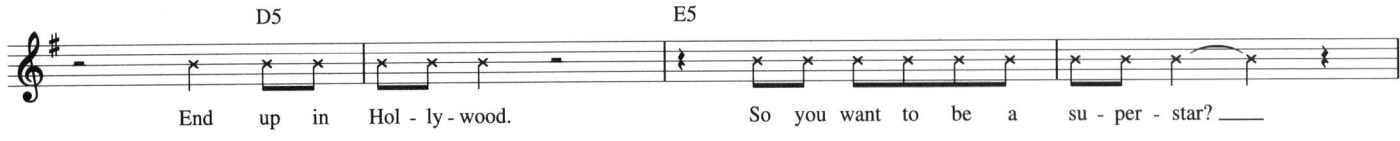
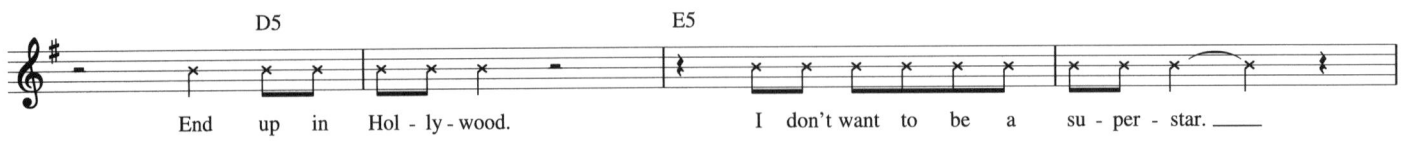

E5
D5
Hol - ly - wood.
I don't want to be a su - per - star.
Free time
Bkgd. Voc.: Crying and sobbing till end
Spoken: Money, power, and fame.
E5
Gtr. 4
grad. bend
1/2
1
1 1/2
1
Gtr. 3
grad. bend
1/2
3/4
1
Gtr. 3
Gtr. 4 tacet
Money, power, and fame.
Laughter: Ha, ha, ha, ha, ha, ha, ha, ha, ha, ha, ha, ha, ha, ha, ha, ha, ha.
Money, power, and fame.

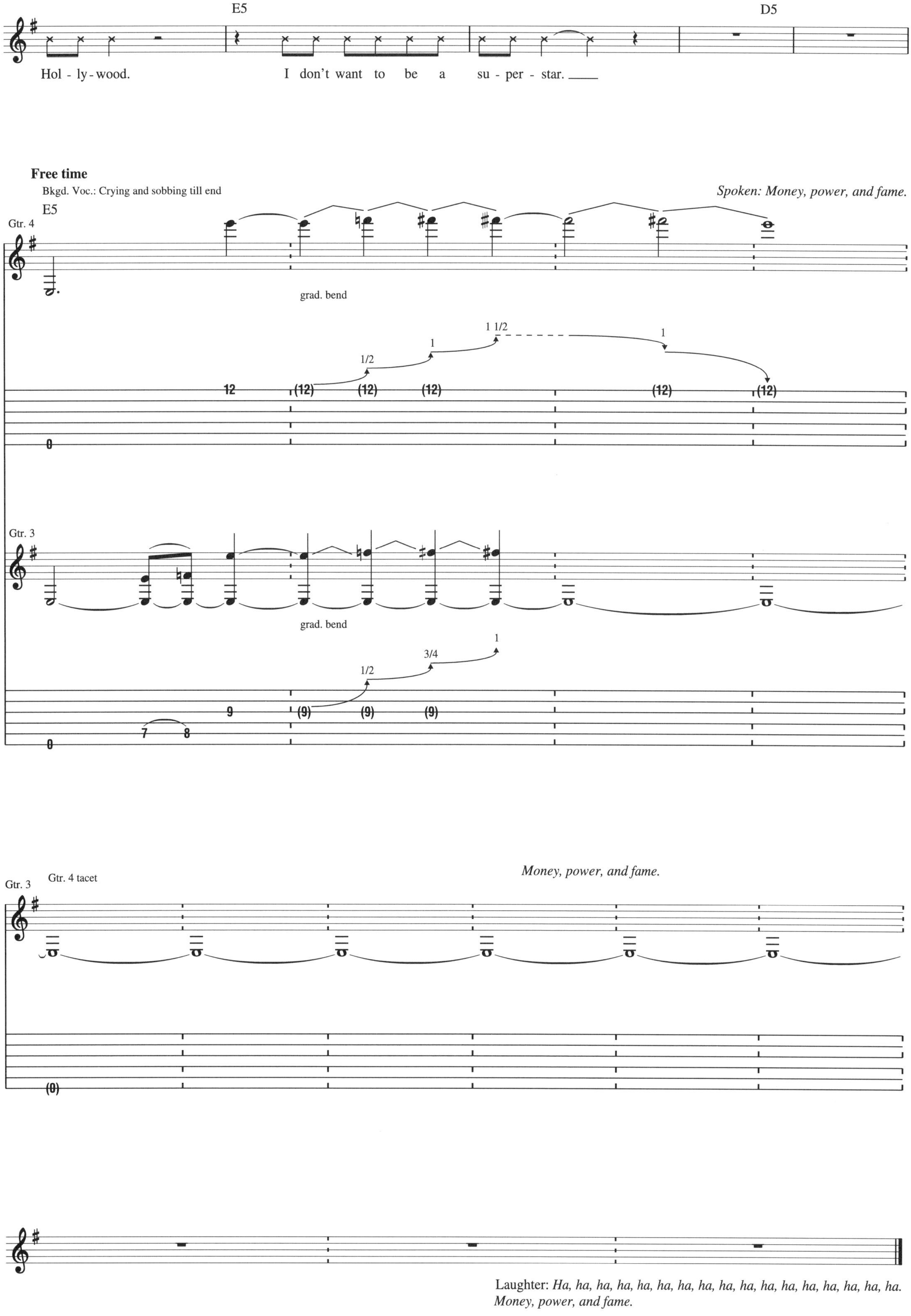

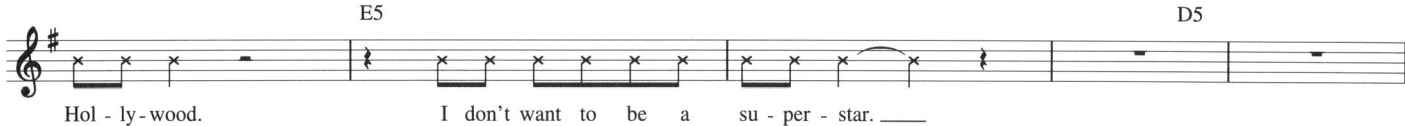

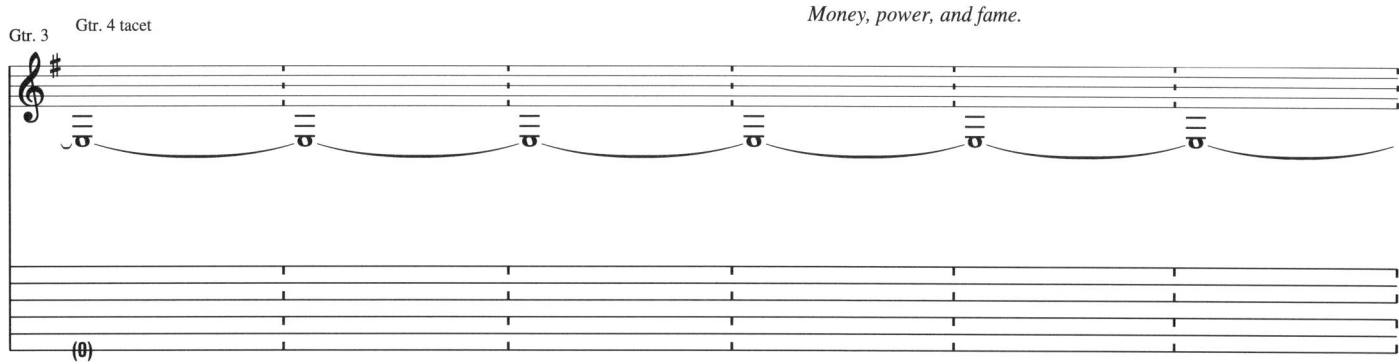

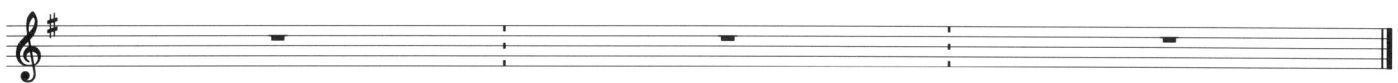

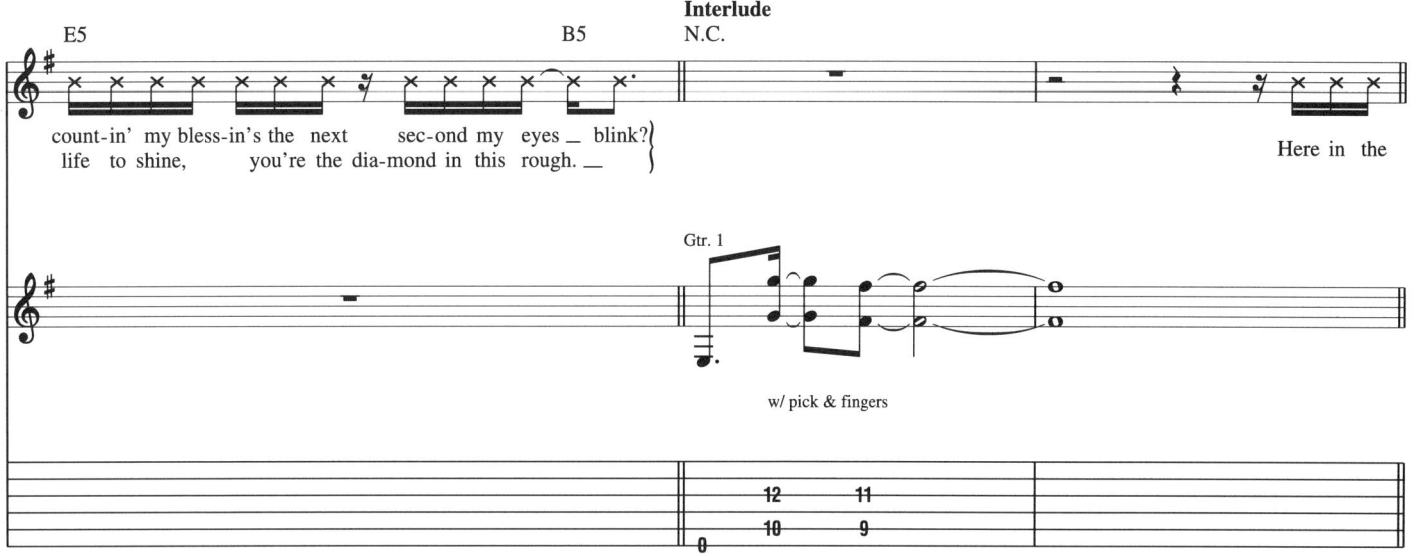

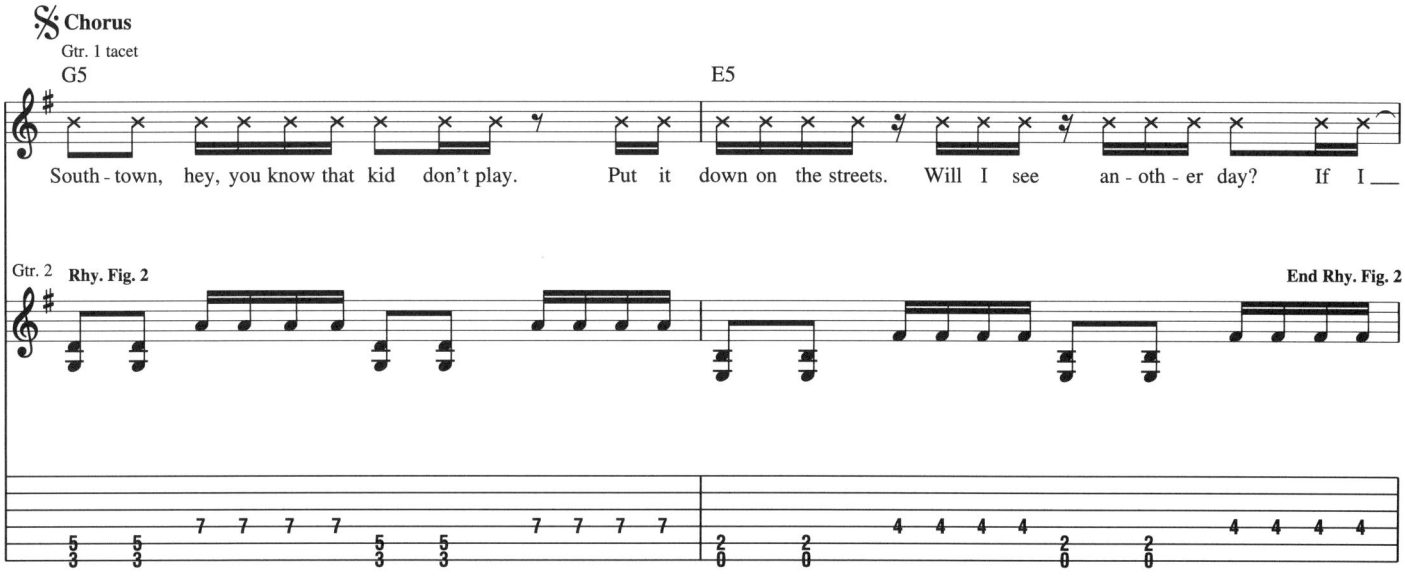

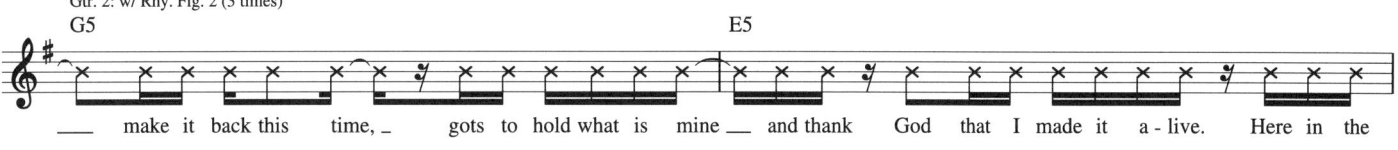

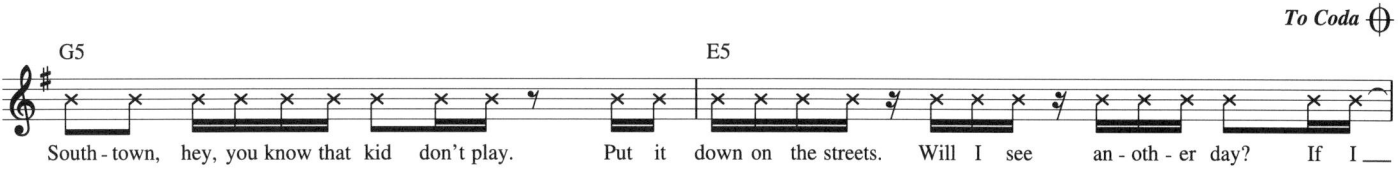

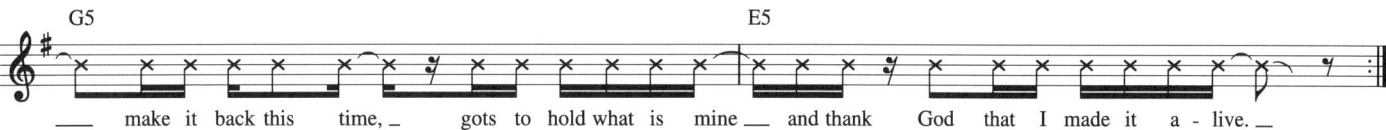

19

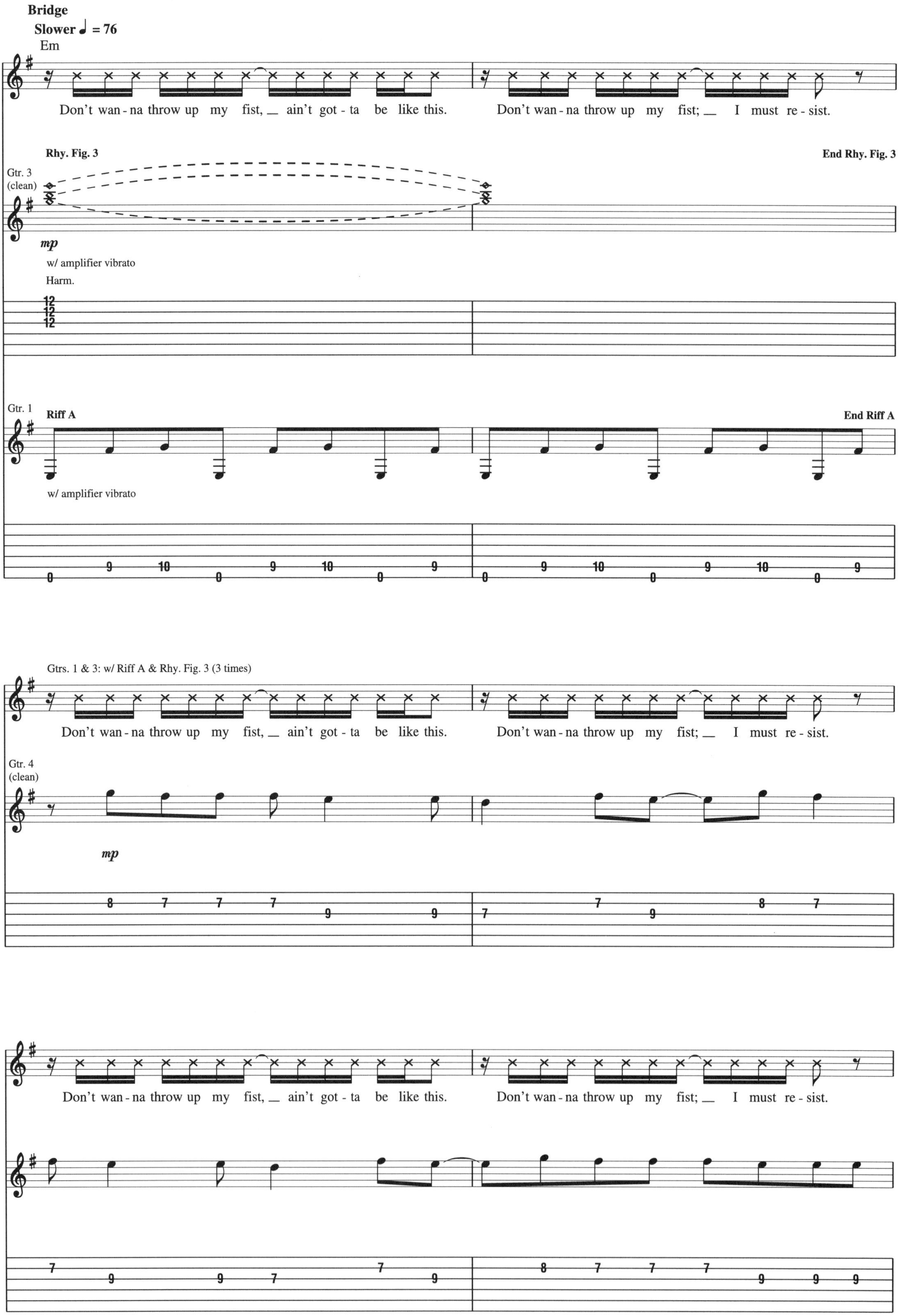
Bridge
Slower ♩ = 76
Em
Don't wan - na throw up my fist, ain't got - ta be like this. Don't wan - na throw up my fist; I must re - sist.
Rhy. Fig. 3
End Rhy. Fig. 3
Gtr. 3 (clean)
mp
w/ amplifier vibrato
Harm.
Gtr. 1
Riff A
End Riff A
w/ amplifier vibrato
Gtrs. 1 & 3: w/ Riff A & Rhy. Fig. 3 (3 times)
Don't wan - na throw up my fist, ain't got - ta be like this. Don't wan - na throw up my fist; I must re - sist.
Gtr. 4 (clean)
mp
Don't wan - na throw up my fist, ain't got - ta be like this. Don't wan - na throw up my fist; I must re - sist.

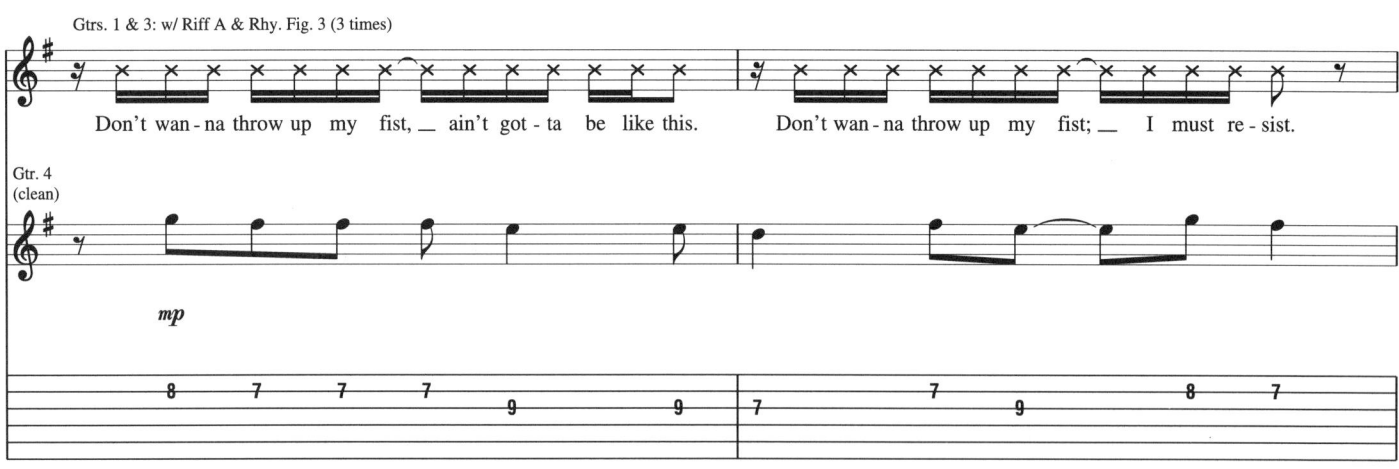

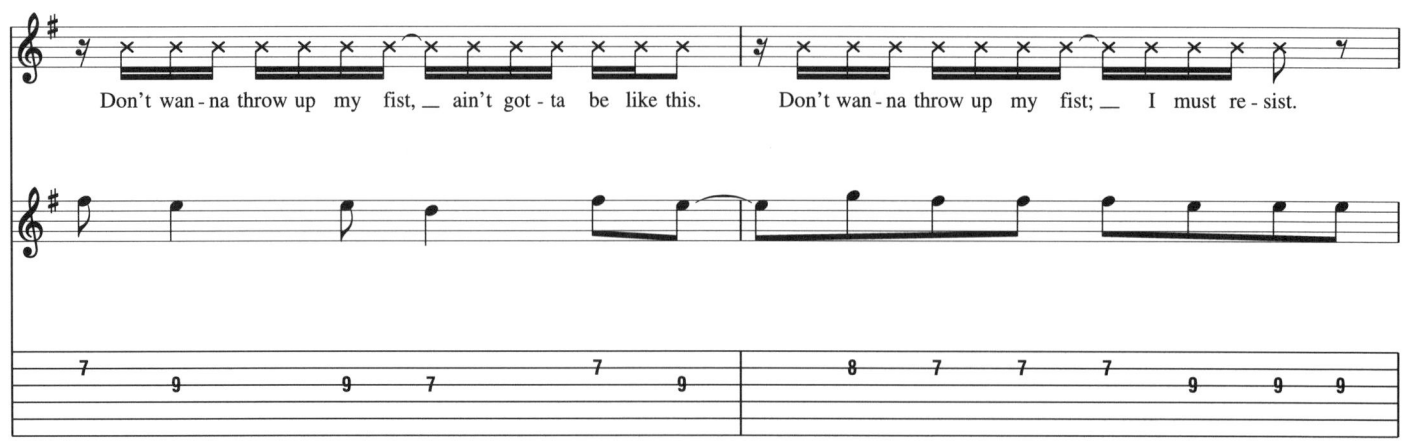

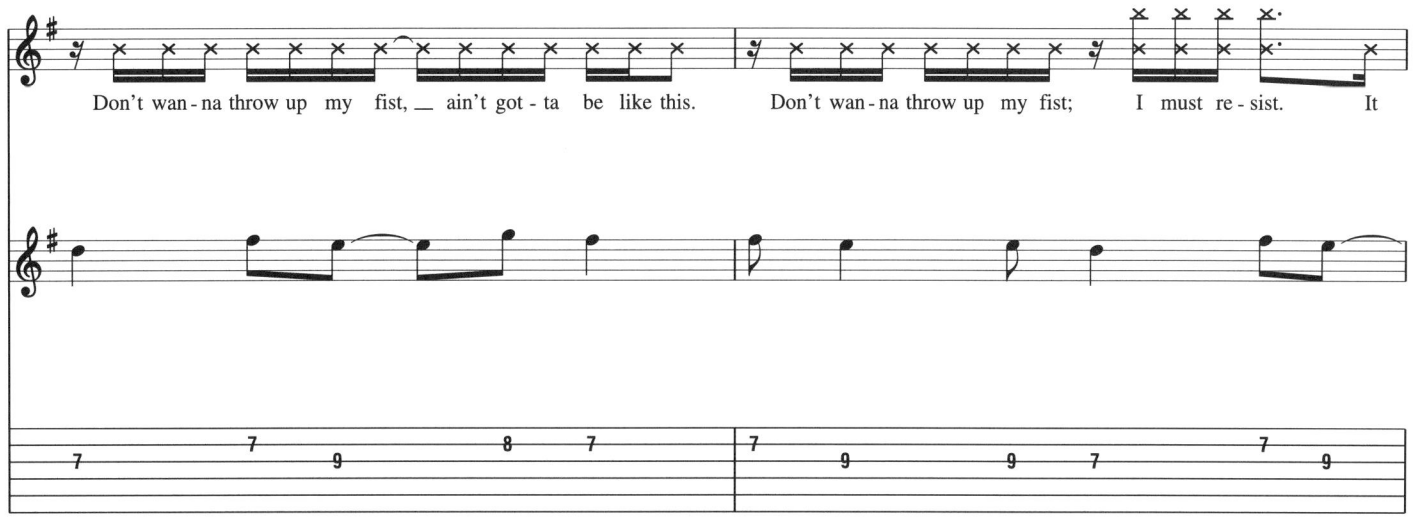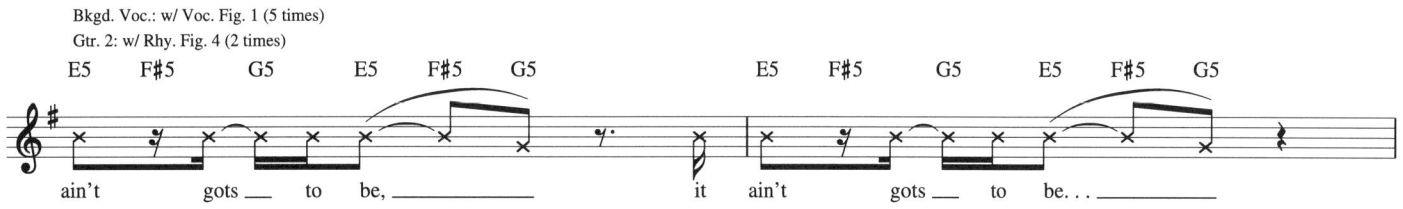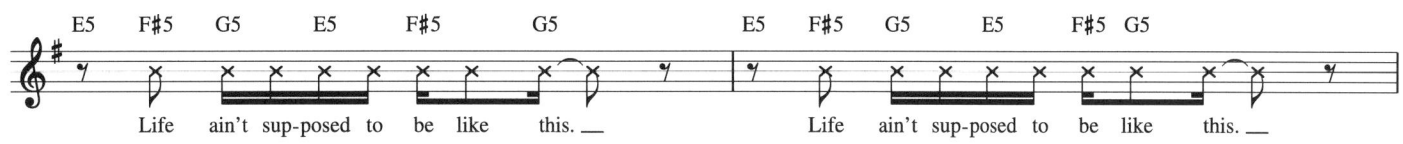

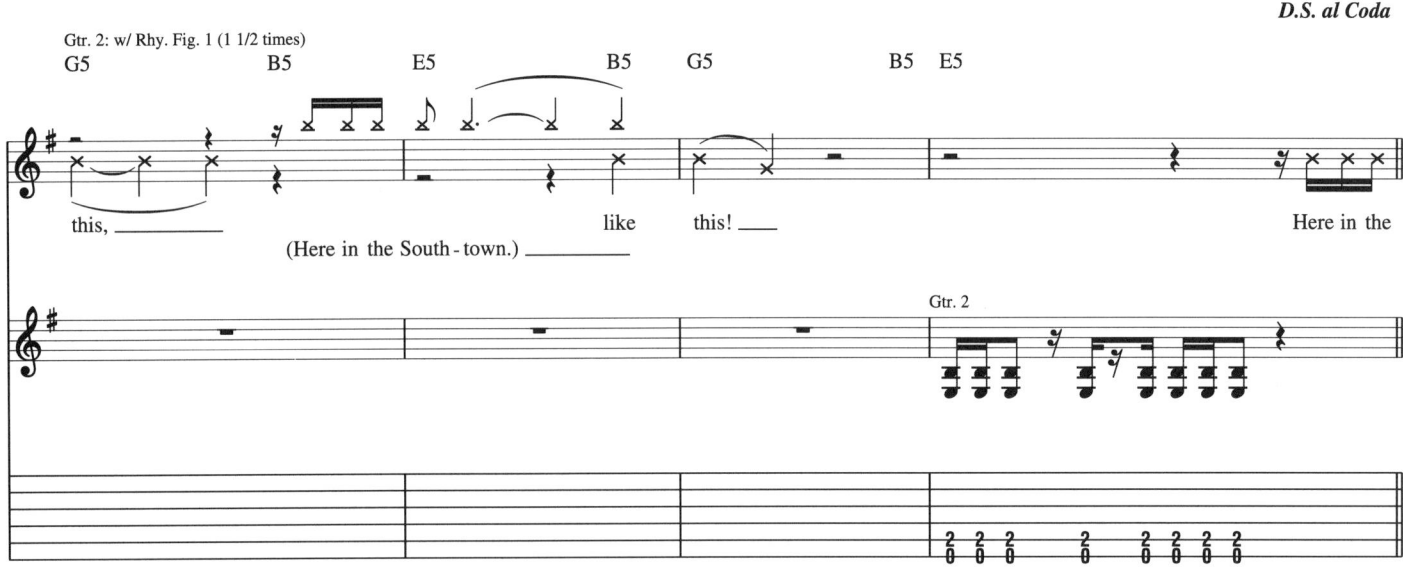
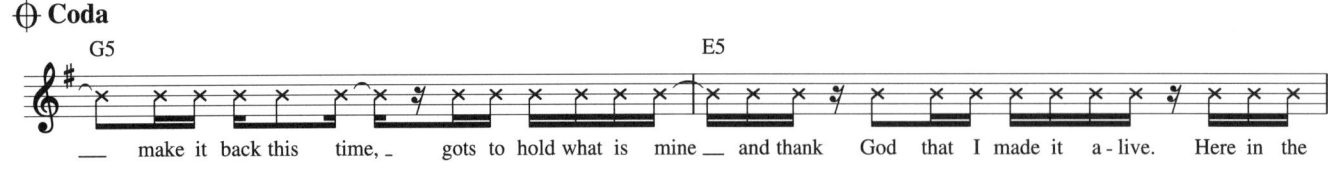
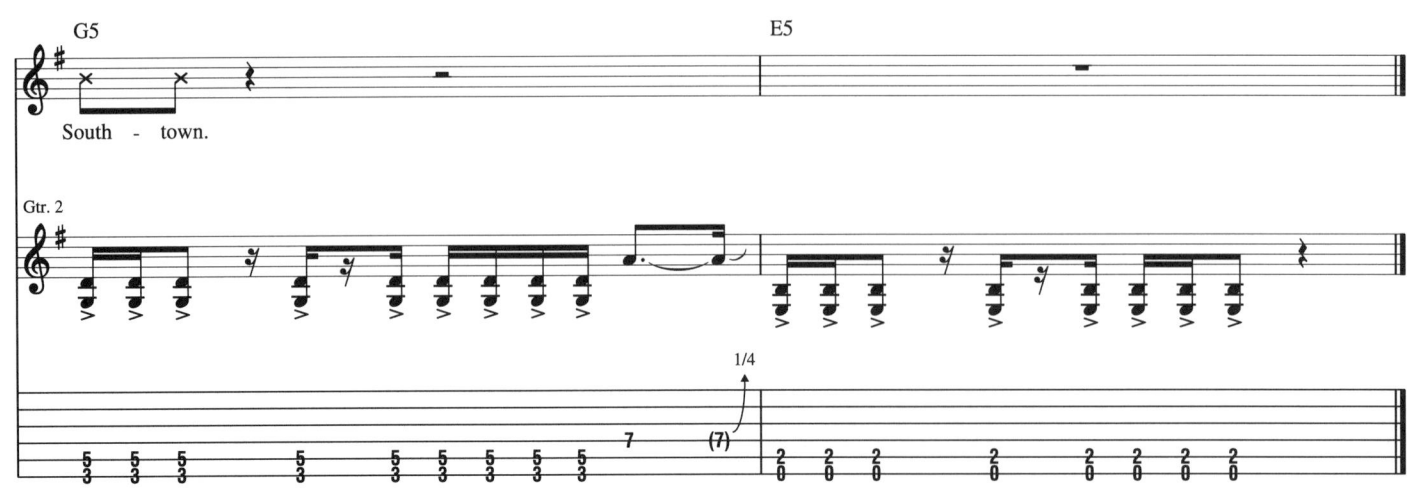

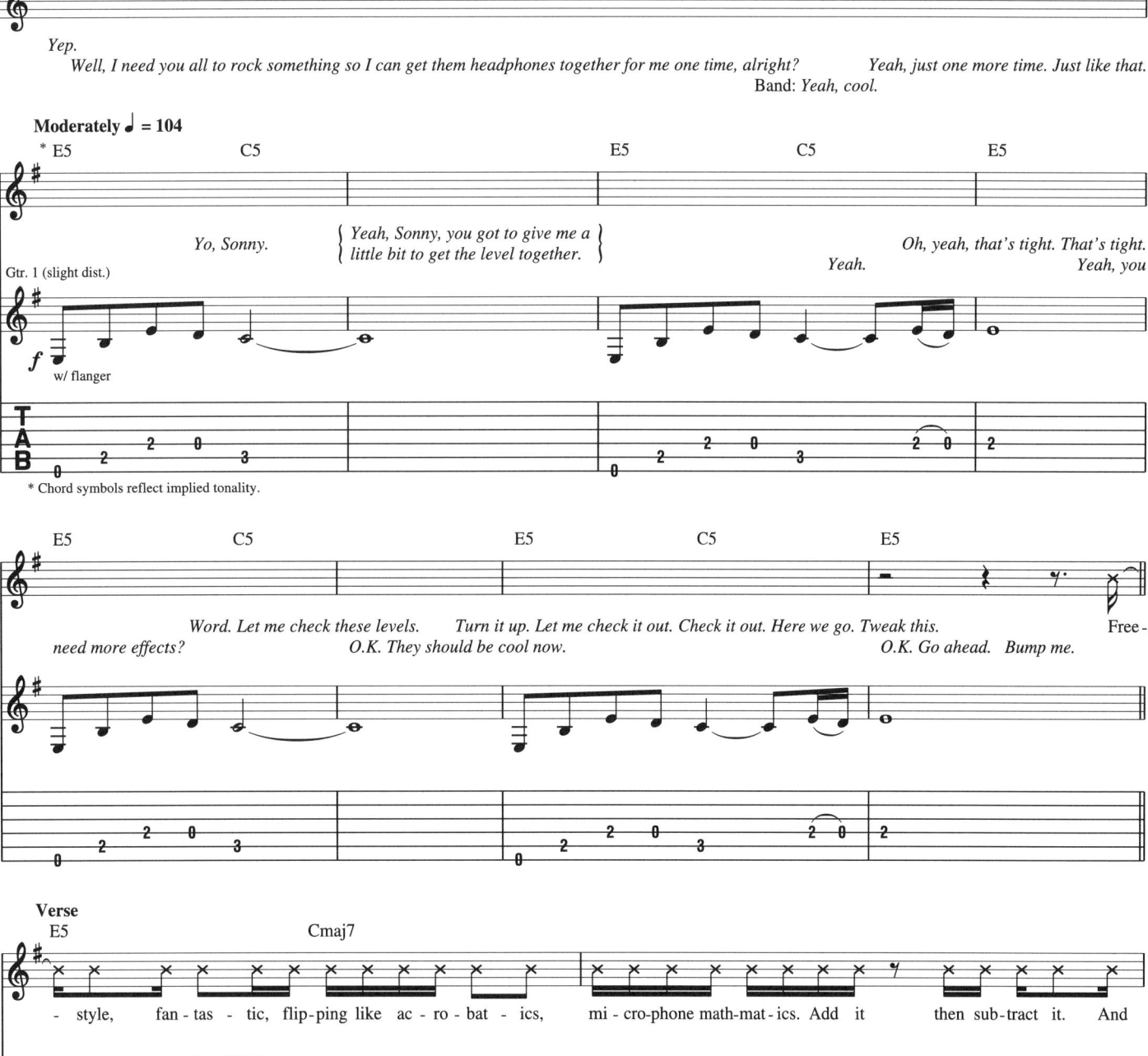

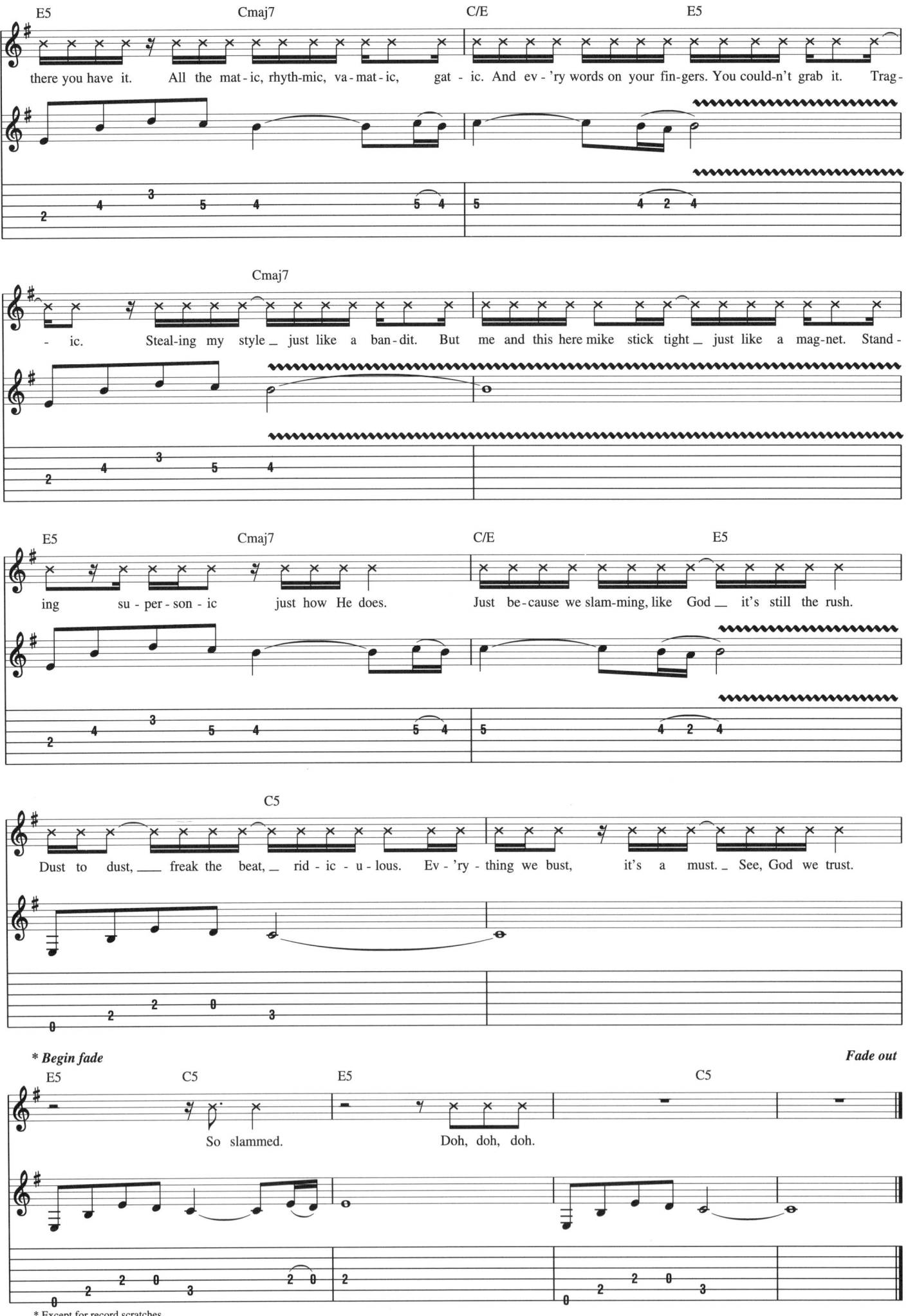

Rock the Party (Off the Hook)

Words and Music by Sonny, Marcos, Traa and Wuv

Tune down 1 step:
(low to high) D–G–C–F–A–D

Intro
Moderately ♩ = 126

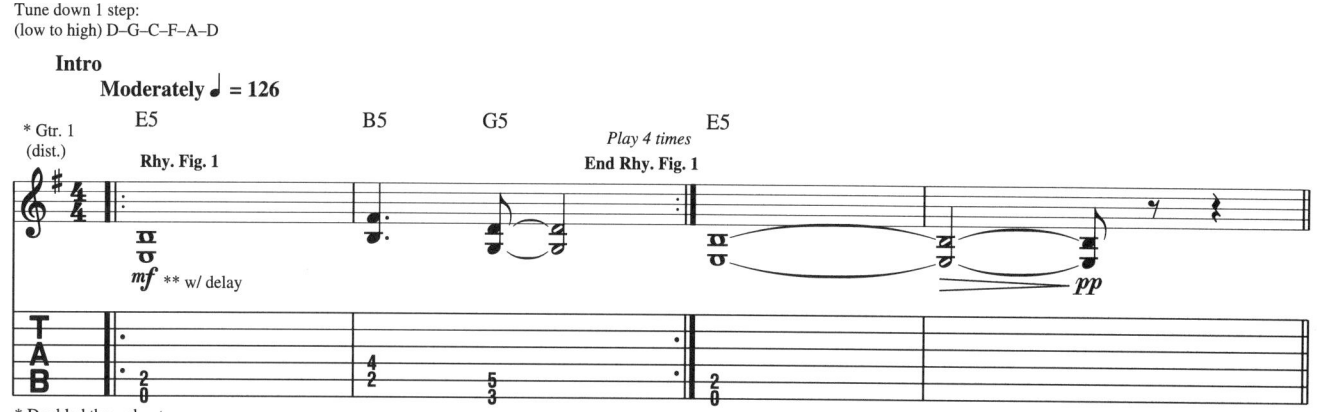

* Doubled throughout
** Set for eigth-note regeneration w/ multiple repeats.

% Verse
Gtr. 1: w/ Rhy. Fig. 1 (4 times)

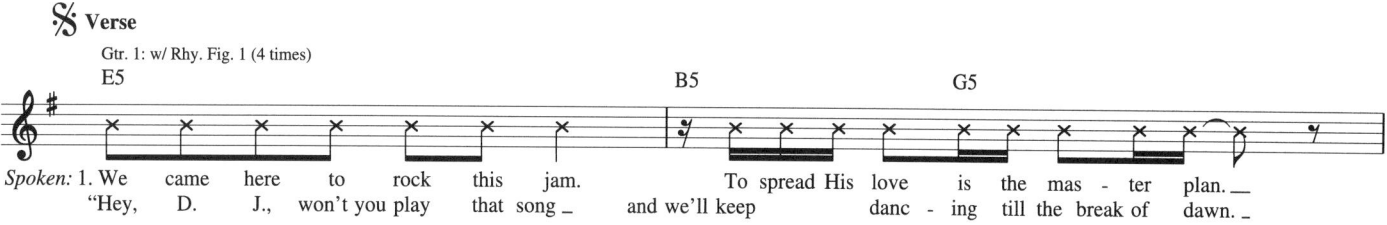

Spoken: 1. We came here to rock this jam. To spread His love is the master plan.
"Hey, D. J., won't you play that song and we'll keep dancing till the break of dawn.

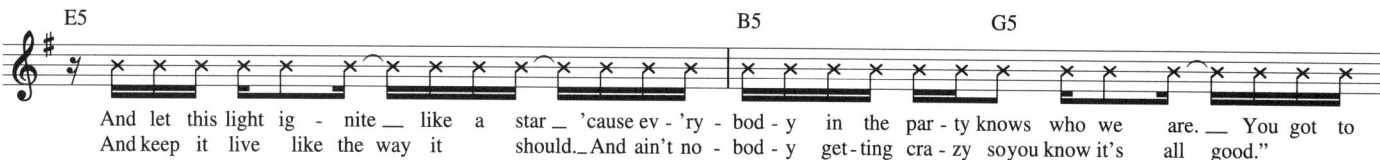

And let this light ignite like a star 'cause ev'rybody in the party knows who we are. You got to
And keep it live like the way it should. And ain't nobody getting crazy so you know it's all good."

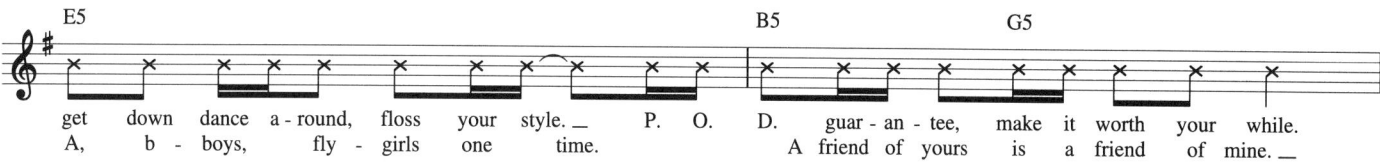

get down dance around, floss your style. P. O. D. guarantee, make it worth your while.
A, b-boys, fly-girls one time. A friend of yours is a friend of mine.

Bad vibes, leave them at the door. Soul checking, house wrecking, keep them begging for more.
Don't bother stoping till this jam is through, 'cause if you've been here before then you know how we do.

Copyright © 1999 by Souljah Music and Famous Music Corporation
International Copyright Secured   All Rights Reserved

Chorus

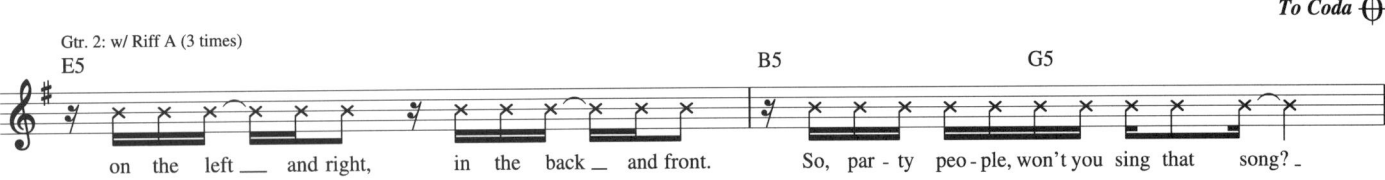

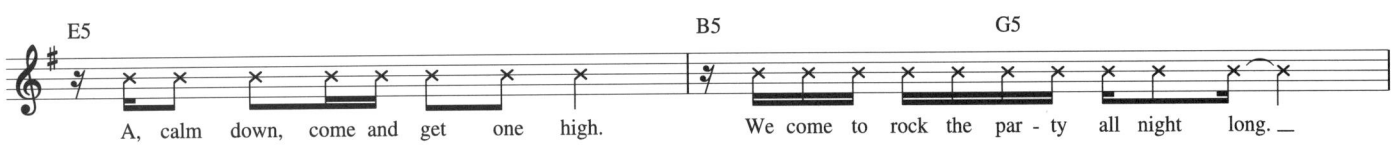

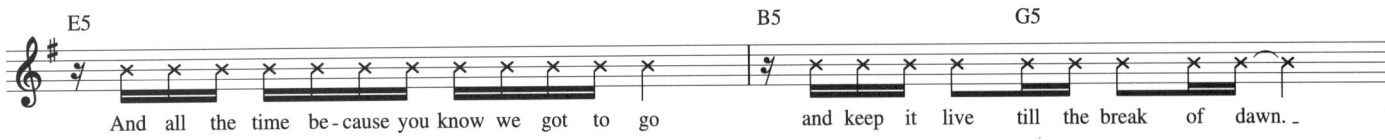

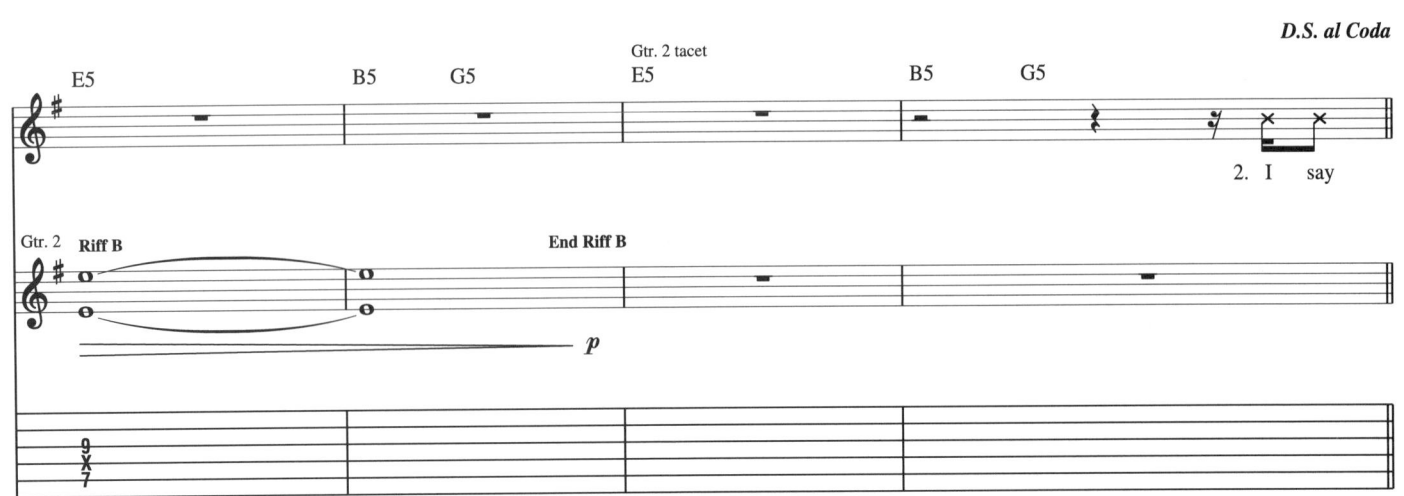

26

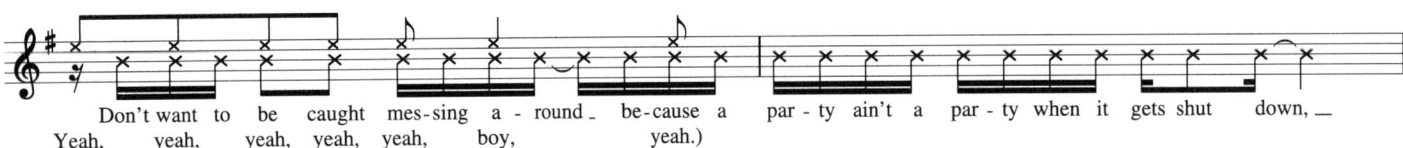

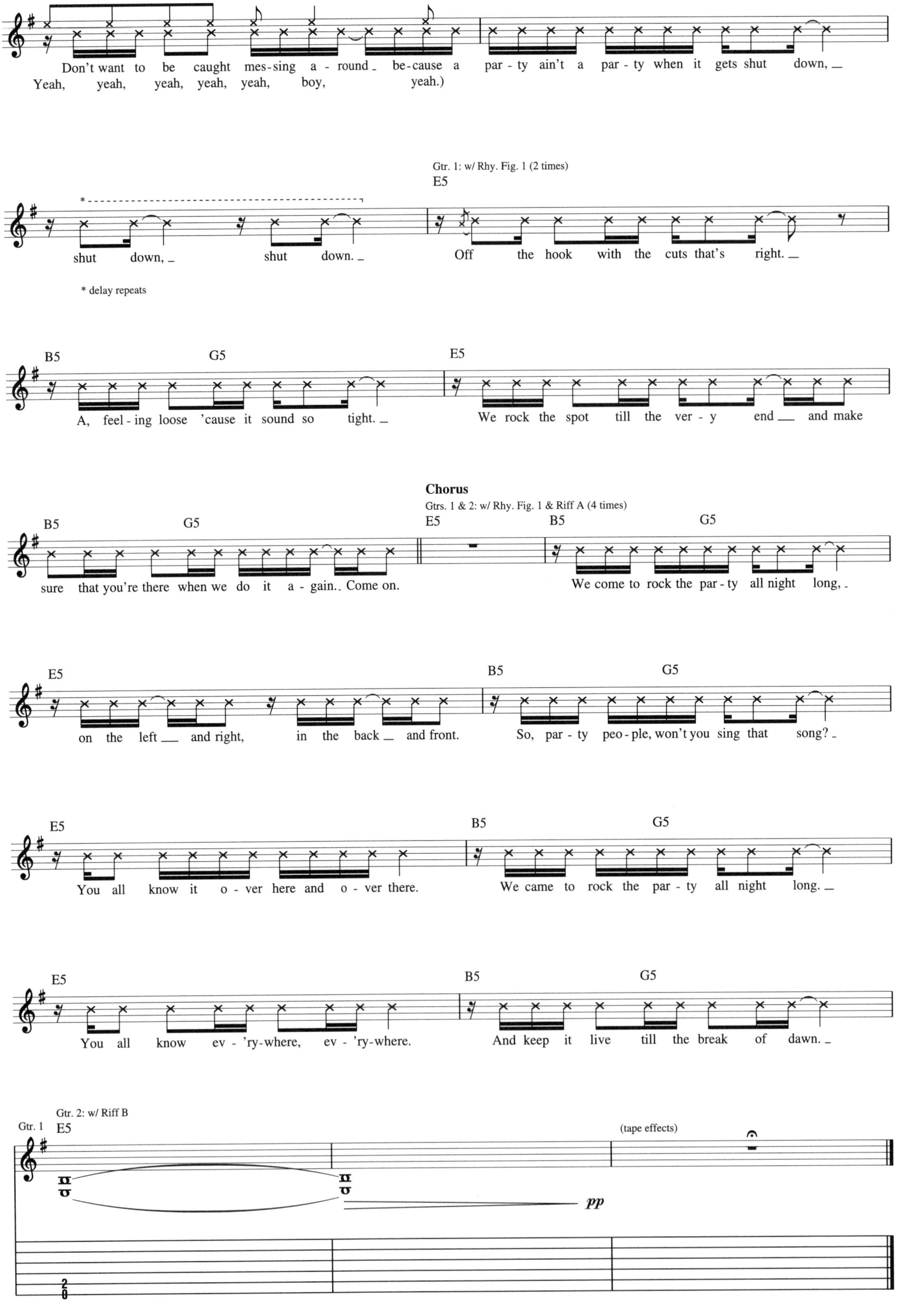
Don't want to be caught mes-sing a-round because a par-ty ain't a par-ty when it gets shut down,
Yeah, yeah, yeah, yeah, yeah, boy, yeah.)
shut down, shut down.
* delay repeats
Gtr. 1: w/ Rhy. Fig. 1 (2 times)
E5
Off the hook with the cuts that's right.
B5 G5
A, feel-ing loose 'cause it sound so tight.
E5
We rock the spot till the ver-y end and make
B5 G5
sure that you're there when we do it a-gain. Come on.
Chorus
Gtrs. 1 & 2: w/ Rhy. Fig. 1 & Riff A (4 times)
E5 B5 G5
We come to rock the par-ty all night long,
E5
on the left and right, in the back and front.
B5 G5
So, par-ty peo-ple, won't you sing that song?
E5
You all know it o-ver here and o-ver there.
B5 G5
We came to rock the par-ty all night long.
E5
You all know ev-'ry-where, ev-'ry-where.
B5 G5
And keep it live till the break of dawn.
Gtr. 2: w/ Riff B
Gtr. 1
E5
(tape effects)
pp

Lie Down

Words and Music by Sonny, Marcos, Traa and Wuv

Tune down 1 step:
(low to high) D–G–C–F–A–D

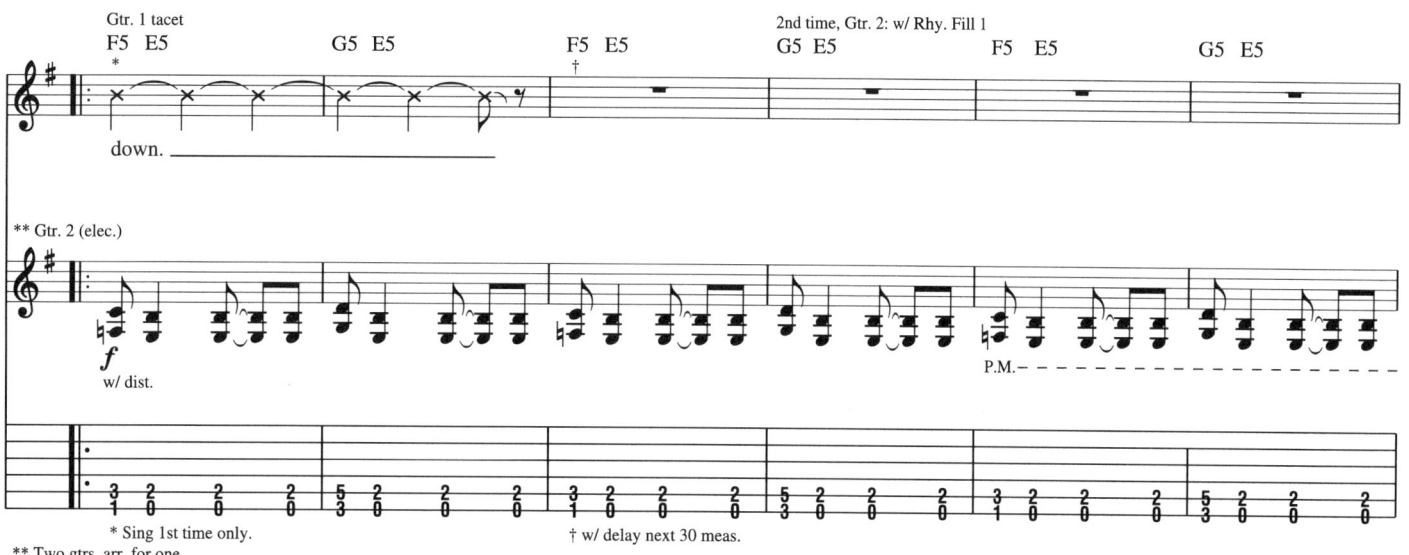

* Sing 1st time only.
** Two gtrs. arr. for one.
† w/ delay next 30 meas.

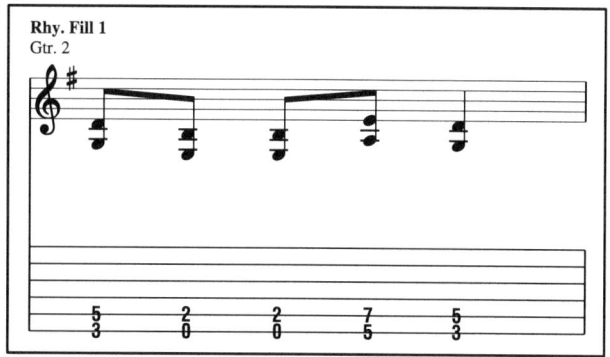

Copyright © 1999 by Souljah Music and Famous Music Corporation
International Copyright Secured   All Rights Reserved

29

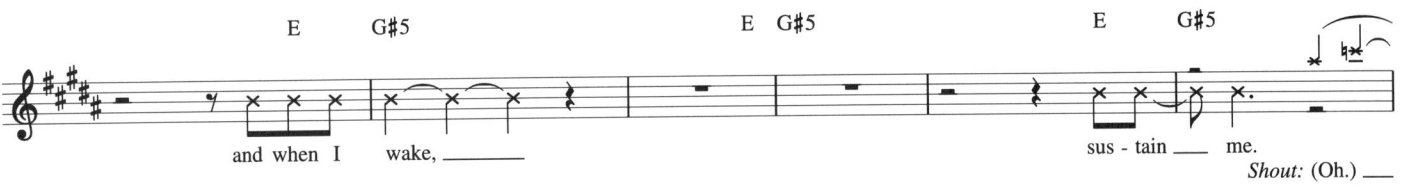
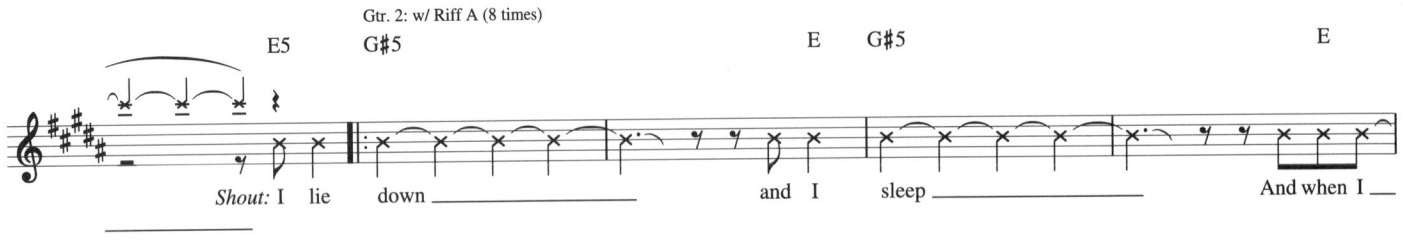
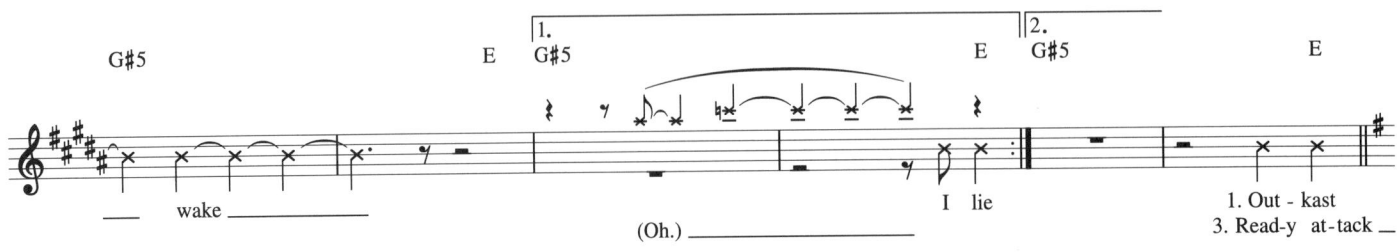

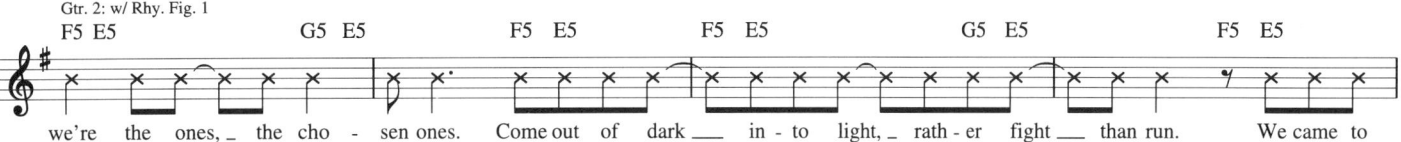
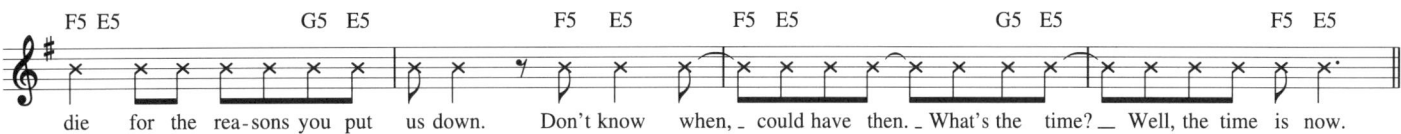

Chorus

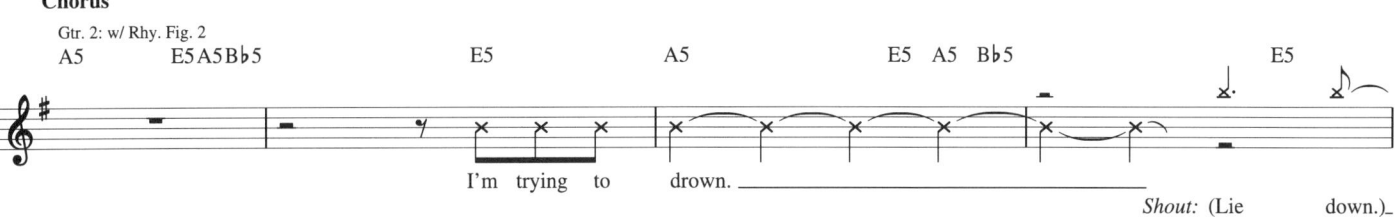

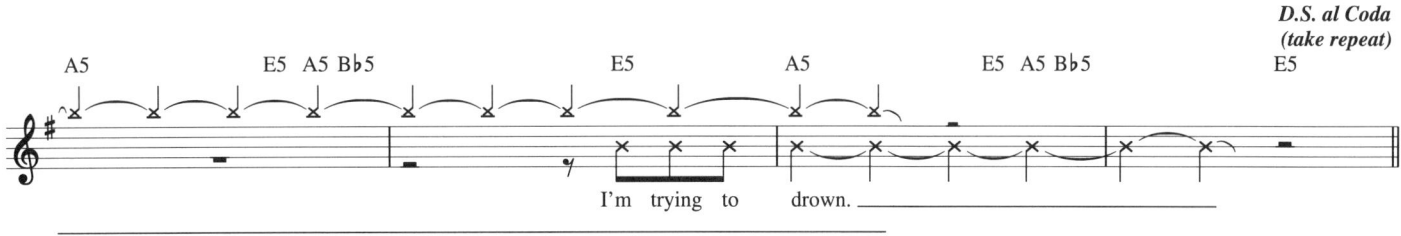

Coda

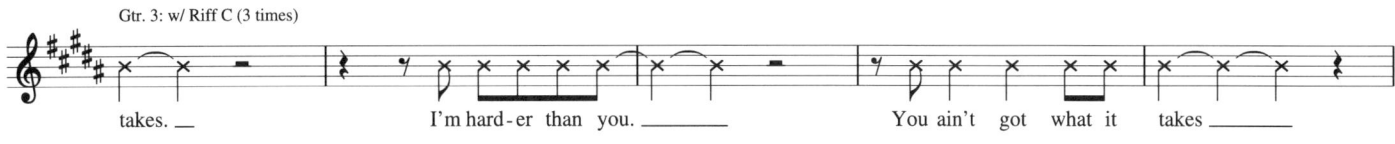
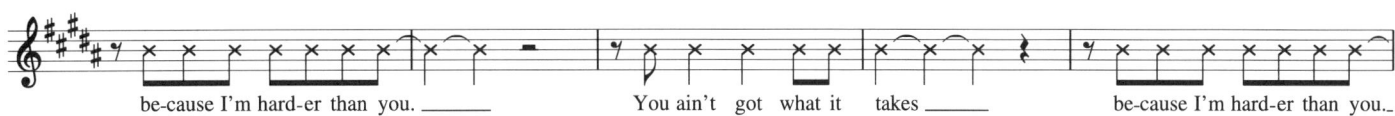

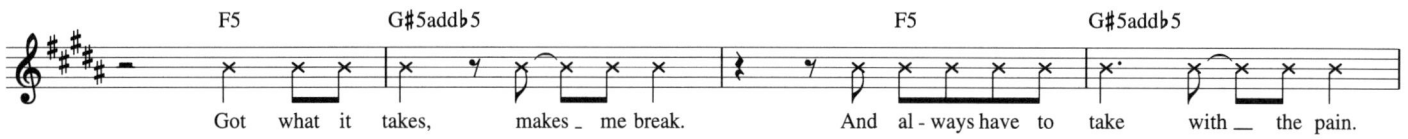
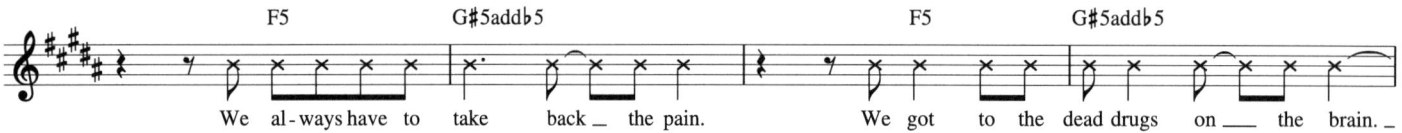

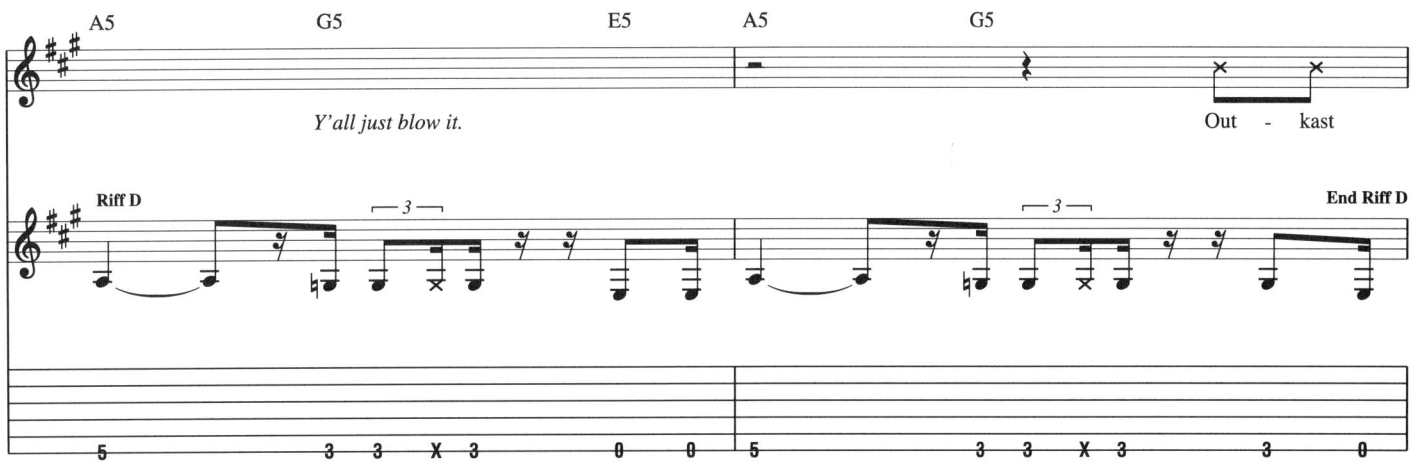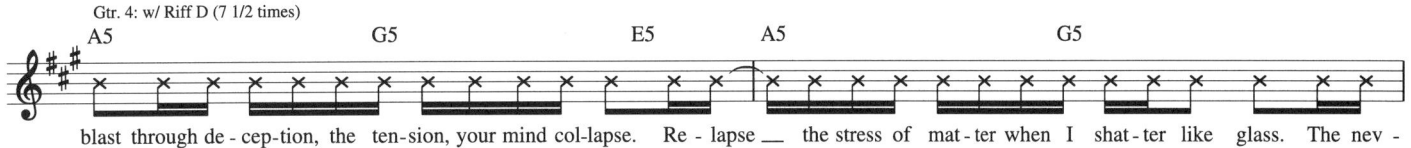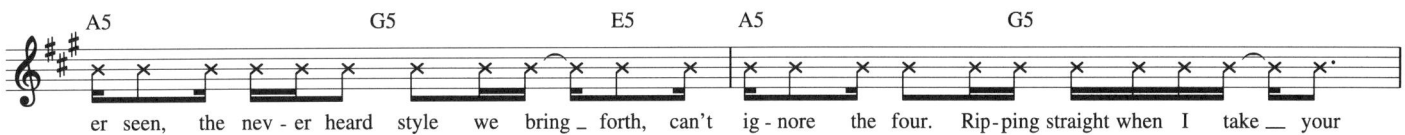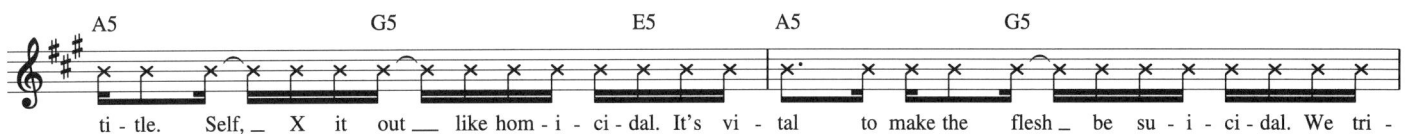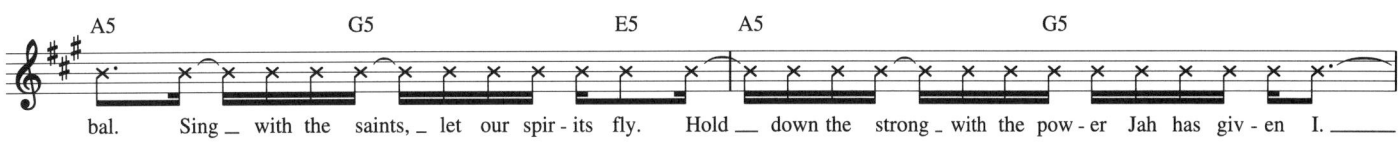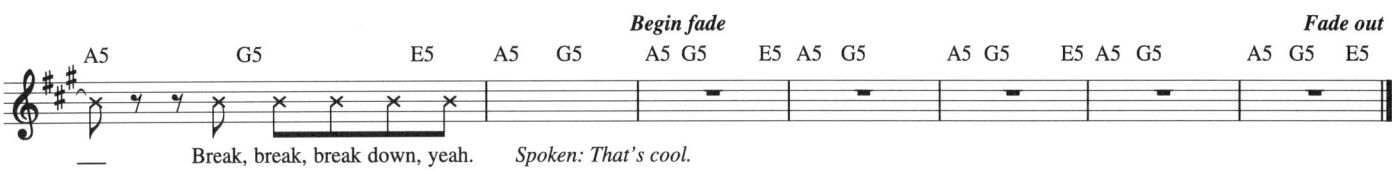

Set Your Eyes to Zion

Words and Music by Sonny, Marcos, Traa and Wuv

Tune down 1 step:
(low to high) D–G–C–F–A–D

Intro
Moderately fast ♩ = 135

Hey, Mr. Deadman, rejoice!

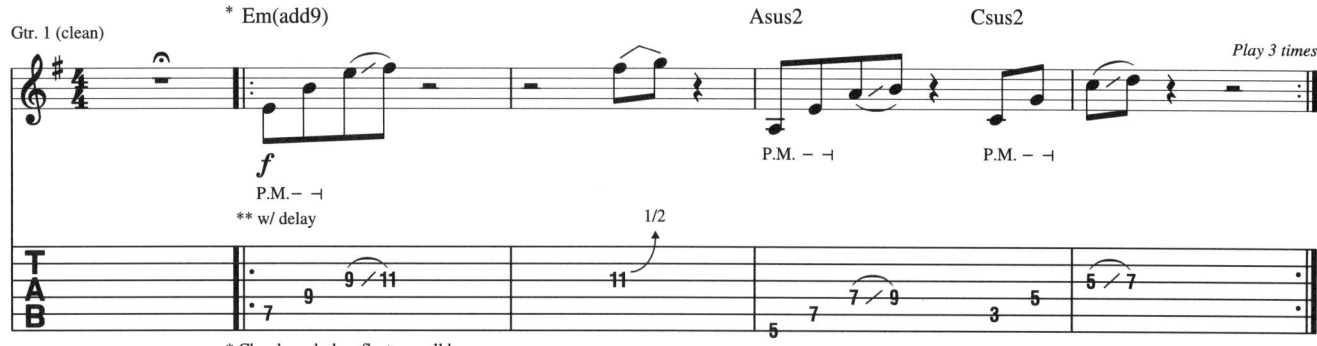

* Chord symbols reflect overall harmony.
** Set for eighth-note regeneration w/ 4 repeats.

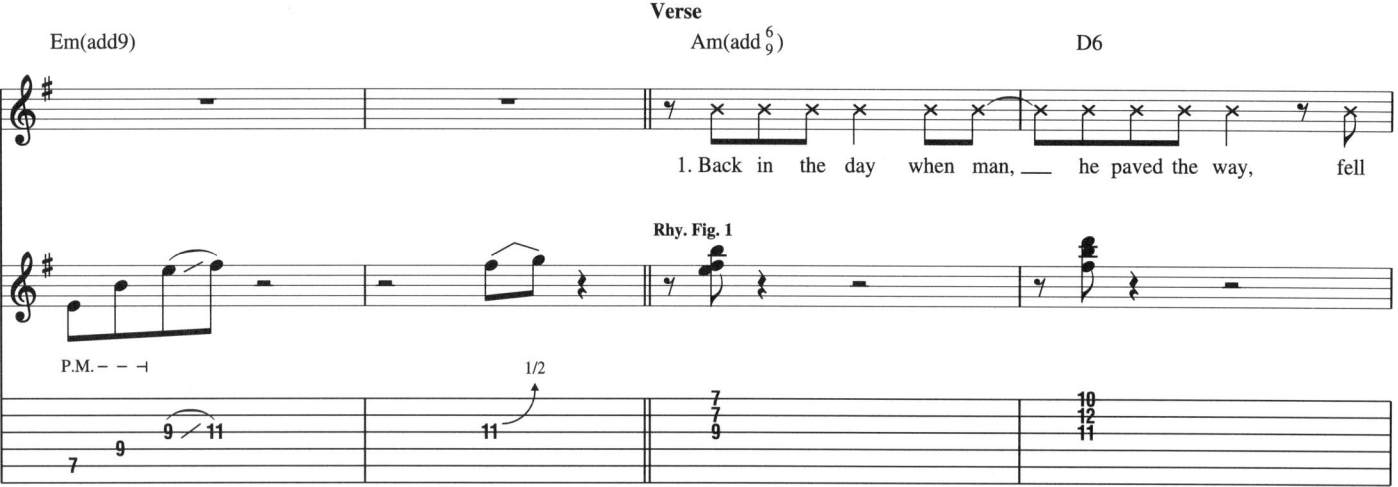

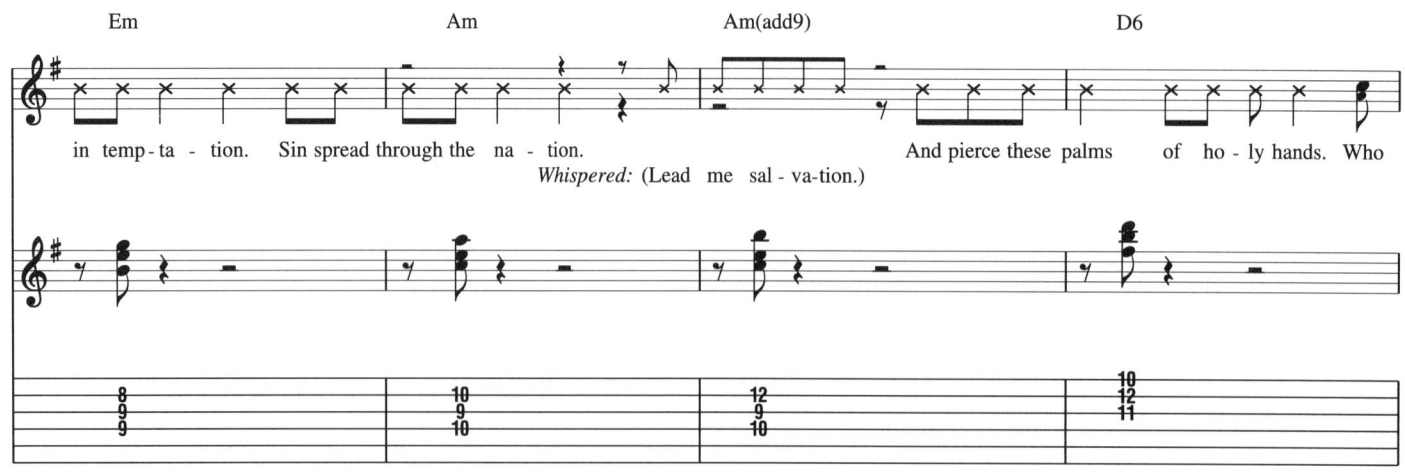

Copyright © 1999 by Souljah Music and Famous Music Corporation
International Copyright Secured   All Rights Reserved

Em
Am
Am(add6/9)
D6
is the son of man? Take me to the prom-ised land where I and I is free. Jah set my mind at ease.
Em7
Am
Am(add9)
Well, I stay cool in the shade e-ven at nine-ty six de-grees. You must be-lieve
D6
Em7
Am
and plant this seed of wis-dom. Stick to the track and don't be trapped by Bab-y-lon.
End Rhy. Fig. 1
Chorus
Am(add9)
Em
Set your eyes to Zi-on. Jah Jah peo-ple ride on.
Riff A
End Riff A
P.M.
P.M.

Gtr. 1: w/ Riff A
Am(add9)
Em
Set your eyes to Zi - on.
Jah Jah peo - ple ride on.
Verse
Gtr. 1: w/ Rhy. Fig. 1
Am(add6/9)
D6
Em
2. For - give them, Lord, for they not know not what they do. Peo -
Am
Am(add9)
D6
ple blame it on you. Can't un - der - stand why dem so mad.
Em
Am
Am(add6/9)
Dem heart get cold, emp - ty with no soul.
Well, I've be - gun.
D6
Em7
Am
To search for One, giv - er of life. I and I rec - og - nize
Am(add9)
D6
Em7
Am
to be with You in par - a - dise. Zi - on I set my eyes.
Whispered: (For - ev - er I'll be with You.)
Chorus
Gtr. 1: w/ Riff A (3 times)
Am(add9)
Em
Set your eyes to Zi - on. Jah Jah peo - ple ride on.
Am(add9)
Em
We set our eyes to Zi - on. Jah Jah peo - ple ride on.

Am(add9)
Em
To Coda
We set our eyes to Zi - on.
Jah Jah peo - ple ride on.
Gtr. 1
P.M.
Gtr. 2 (clean)
mf
Gtr. 1
divisi
w/ delay
Guitar Solo
Gtr. 1 tacet
Am(add 6/9)
Gtr. 2
Em7
Gtr. 3 (clean)
mf
w/ delay & chorus
let ring throughout
Am(add 6/9)
Em7
1/2
1/2
1/2

Verse

Gtr. 1: w/ Rhy. Fig. 1
Gtrs. 2 & 3 tacet

3. Tell me, Mister Deadman, do you have the answer? How can you get to heaven? Do you have the answer?

Hey, Mister Deadman, I'll tell you if you want to know how

D.S. al Coda
(take repeat)

you can get to heaven. Believe in I Jah Jah, son.

Coda
Outro
Em7
Bm7
Am7
on. Ride on.
(On.)
We ride on.
You got to ride
Gtr. 1
Rhy. Fig. 2
End Rhy. Fig. 2
Gtr. 2
Riff B
End Riff B
Gtrs. 1 & 2: w/ Rhy. Fig. 2 & Riff B (2 times)
on.
We ride on.
Jah peo - ple ride on.
Ah, bring it. Ride on.
My sis - ter ride on.

Lo Siento

Words and Music by Sonny, Marcos, Traa and Wuv

Psalm 150

Words and Music by Sonny, Marcos, Traa and Wuv

Tune down 1 step:
(low to high) D–G–C–F–A–D

A Moderately slow ♩ = 99

*Chord symbols reflect basic harmony.

B ** Recitation

** Psalm 150 - Hebrew

Copyright © 1999 by Souljah Music and Famous Music Corporation
International Copyright Secured   All Rights Reserved

43

Cadd9
Gtr. 2: w/ Riff A
Em
Em7
Em
Em7
Em
Em7
End Riff A
Gtr. 1
Em
Em7
Cadd9
Gtr. 1 tacet
Gtr. 2
Em7

Image

Words and Music by Sonny, Marcos, Traa and Wuv

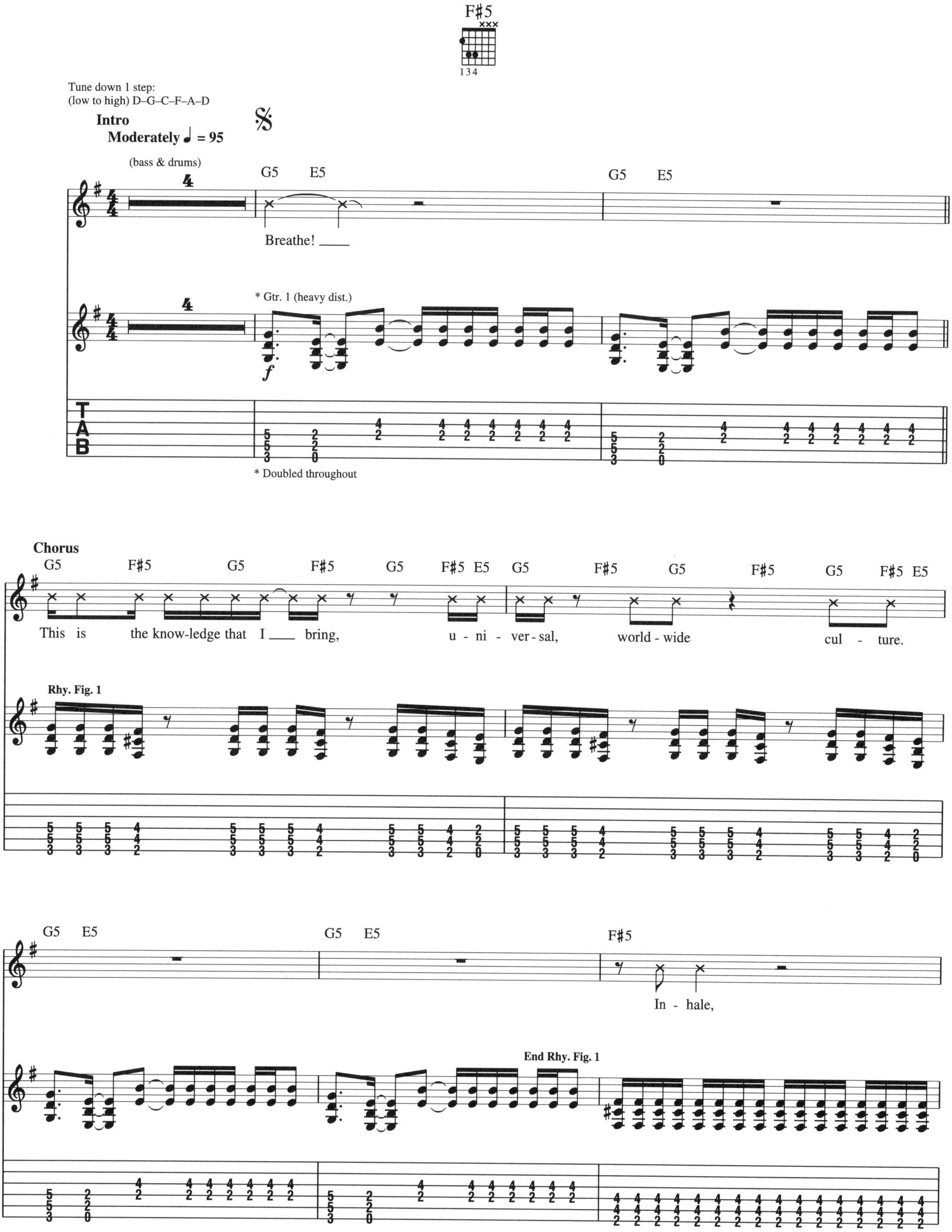

2nd time, Gtr. 2: w/ Rhy. Fill 2
G5 E5
G5 E5
ex - hale, right!
Gtr. 1: w/ Rhy. Fig. 1
G5 F#5 G5 F#5 G5 F#5 E5 G5 F#5 G5 F#5 G5 F#5 E5 G5 E5 G5 E5
This is the know-ledge that I bring, u - ni - ver-sal, world-wide cul - ture. I takes it
Slower ♩ = 70
F#5 G5 E5 F#5 G5 F#5
2nd time, Gtr. 2: w/ Fill 3
G5 E5 F#5 G5
all in. No sec-ond-guess-ing.
Gtr. 2 (dist.)
mf
w/ flanger & panned delay
Gtr. 1
Rhy. Fig. 2
Fill 2
Gtr. 2
P.S.
w/ panned delay
Fill 3
Gtr. 2
8va
P.S.
w/ panned delay

47

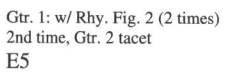

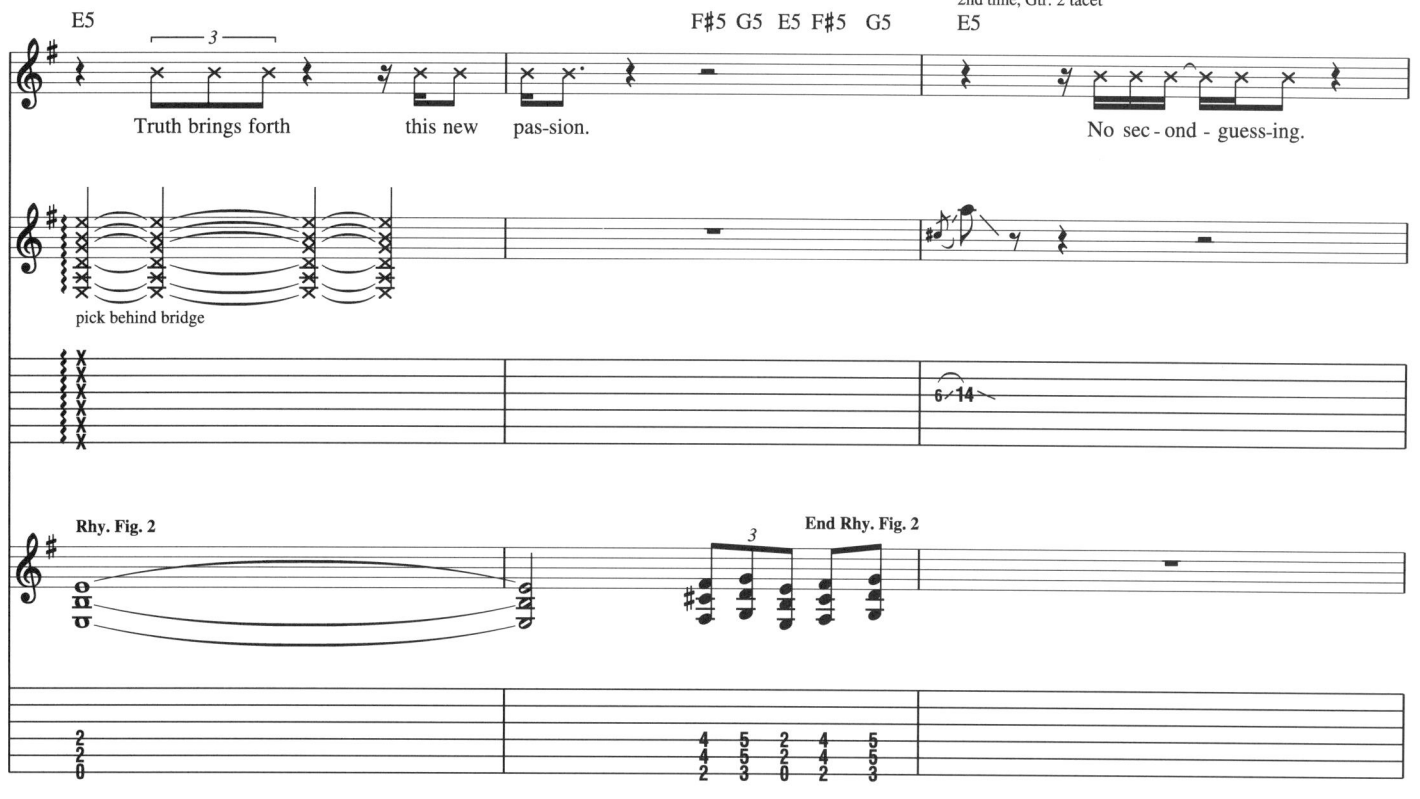

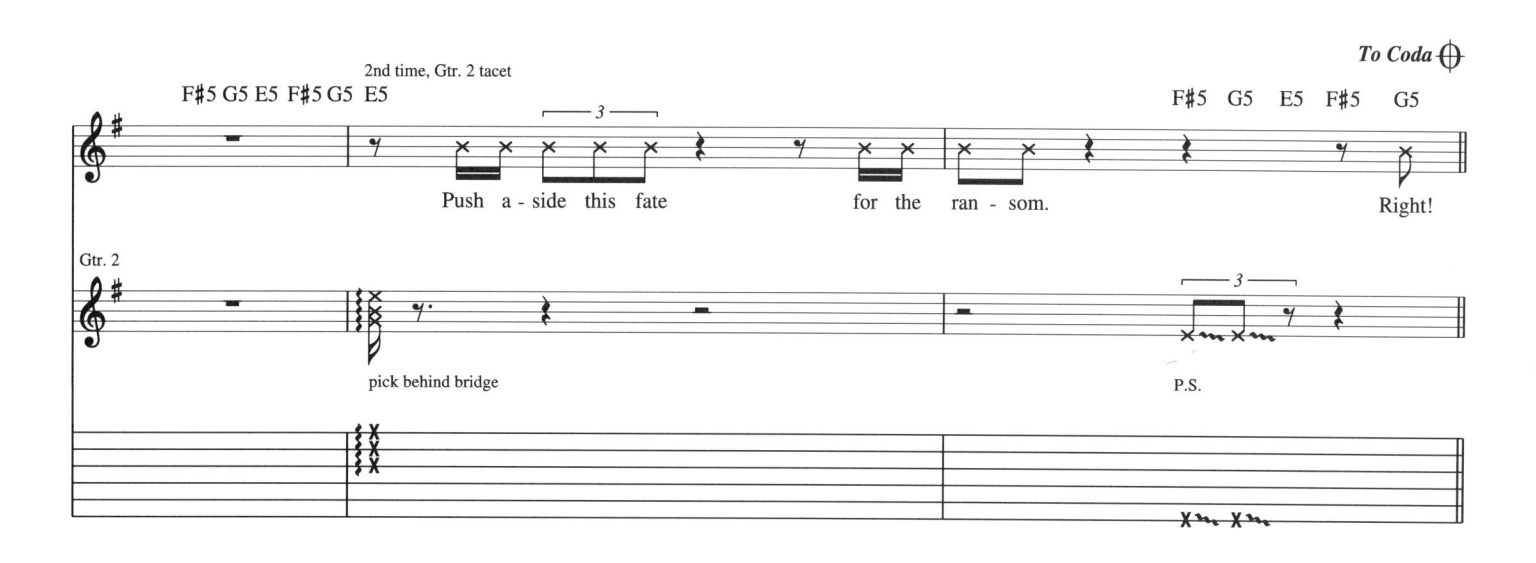

Gtr. 1: w/ Rhy. Fig. 3 (3 times)
F#5 G5 E5 F#5 G5 E5 F#5 G5 F#5 G5 E5
White wool, fire eyes, glow-ing in red.
Shin-ing face, this morn-ing stars re-flec-tions.
Wat-er of rush, plan-et hold, dou-ble edge.
Em-brac-ing light, the clear-ness of sun-rise.
2nd time, Gtr. 2 tacet
F#5 G5 E5 F#5 G5 F#5 G5 E5
Gtr. 2 tacet
2nd time, Gtr. 2: w/ Fill 1
F#5 G5 E5 F#5 G5
Fall-ing down dead, last first, it's one life.
Tow-er strong in this re-fuge my for-tress.
Gtr. 2
pick behind bridge
F#5 G5 E5 F#5 G5 F#5 G5 E5 F#5 G5 F#5
D.S. al Coda
Gtr. 1
accelerando
Coda
F#5
Gtr. 1
Gtr. 2
Fill 1
Gtr. 2
P.S.
flange & delay off

Shouts

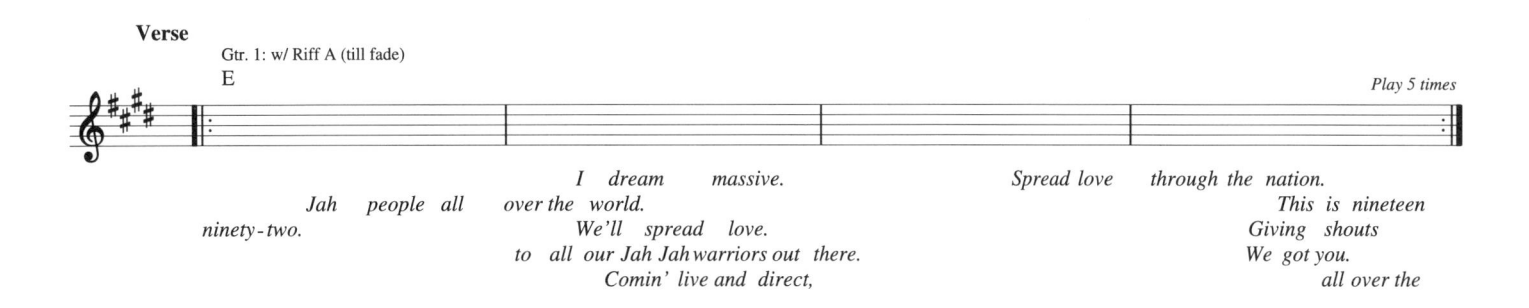

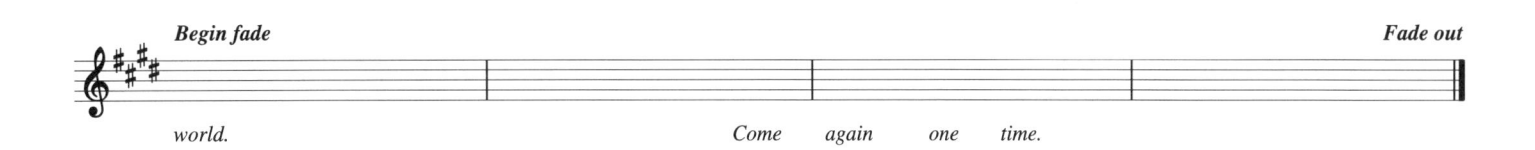

Words and Music by Sonny, Marcos, Traa and Wuv

Tune down 1 step:
(low to high) D–G–C–F–A–D

Intro
Moderate Hip-hop ♩ = 129

Gtr. 1 (clean)

G5   E

Riff A

*Bass arr. for gtr.

End Riff A

Check, check, one, two.

Verse

Gtr. 1: w/ Riff A (till fade)

E

Play 5 times

Jah people all over the world. I dream massive. Spread love through the nation. This is nineteen ninety-two. We'll spread love. Giving shouts to all our Jah Jah warriors out there. We got you. Comin' live and direct, all over the

Begin fade   *Fade out*

world.   Come again one time.

Copyright © 1999 by Souljah Music and Famous Music Corporation
International Copyright Secured   All Rights Reserved

49

Tribal

Words and Music by Sonny, Marcos, Traa and Wuv

Tune down 1 step:
(low to high) D–G–C–F–A–D

Intro
Moderately slow ♩ = 72

* Doubled throughout
** Chord symbols reflect overall harmony.

Chorus
Faster ♩ = 78

Where do you stand in this battle cry, tribal soldier? Represent! I and I ___ Jah Jah warriors.

Copyright © 1999 by Souljah Music and Famous Music Corporation
International Copyright Secured   All Rights Reserved

4.
Verse
Slower ♩ = 73
Gtr. 1 tacet
D5 E5 D5 E5 F♯5 Dmaj9 C♯m/B A/B
Rep-re-sent! I and I.
1. The re-con-struc-tion com-menc-
Gtr. 3 (clean)
End Rhy. Fig. 1
Rhy. Fig. 2
End Rhy. Fig. 2
mf
w/ delay
let ring
Faster ♩ = 76
Gtr. 3: w/ Rhy. Fig. 2 (3 times)
F♯5 Dmaj9 C♯m/B A/B
- es, the sol-diers e-quip for the les - sons. My life a sac - ri - fice is made new through these con - fes - sions. Man - i -
fest - ed, this joy is my de - sire. Light this fire to flames, praise the name, Je - ho - vah Ji - reh.
Is my pro - vid - er the truth that lives in - side of this fight - er? Take me high - er, Mas - ter, Sire, makes me a rid - er.
And I'm a ride on down till I break through the front lines. And ain't go - ing home un - til I gets mines.
Gtr. 3
let ring

CHORUS
Faster ♩ = 78

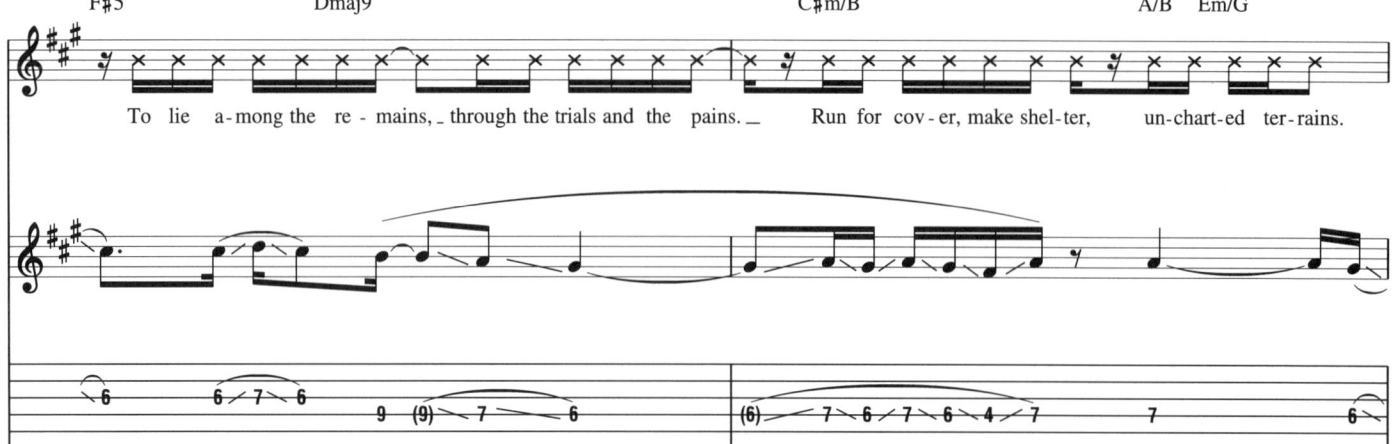

Gtr. 1: w/ Rhy. Fig. 1
Gtr. 3 tacet

Tribal warriors. Where do you stand in this battle cry, tribal soldier?

1., 2., 3.
Represent! I and I ___ Jah Jah warriors.

4.
Represent! I and I. ___

Verse
Gtr. 3: w/ Rhy. Fig. 2 (4 times)

2. I grab a-hold of my second chance, this time gonna make it last. Left the world came back an Outkast.

* Gtr. 4 (clean)

* Backwards gtr.

To lie among the remains, through the trials and the pains. Run for cover, make shelter, uncharted terrains.

52

F♯5 Dmaj9 C♯m/B A/B
Blood stains light the path to the ways of liv - ing breath. And my soul's put to the test next.
F♯5 Dmaj9 C♯m/B A/B
Blessed with the mic in my hand, Jah make straight my steps. So then I hooked up with pay - a - ble on death.
Faster ♩ = 82
Gtr. 4 tacet
F♯5 Dsus2 Bsus 2/4
We flow in u - ni - ty, stand in one while the fool - ish be. Lost in this hour, with pow - er we have au - thor - i - ty.
Gtr. 3 Riff A
End Riff A
* w/ delay & dist.
* Set for sixteenth-note regeneration with multiple repeats.
Gtr. 3: w/ Riff A (3 times)
F♯5 Dsus2 Bsus 2/4
To o - ver - come while these cow - ards just pick up and run. But we ain't done till the bat - tle's been fought and won.
F♯5 Dsus2 Bsus 2/4
This vic - tor - y, how sweet it be, is al - read - y ours. Hold - ing the stars is the man that car - ries my scars.

F♯5 Dsus2 Bsus 2/4 E5
Al-ways the same, wear his name with no __ shame. Here in this bat-tle cry, we will nev-er die.
Whispered: (We will
Gtr. 1
P.M.
Bridge
F♯5 E5 F5 G5 A5 E5 F♯5 E5 F5 G5 A5 E5
Voc. Fig. 1
We will nev-er die.
nev-er die. We will nev-er die. We will
P.M.
F♯5 E5 F5 G5 A5 E5 F♯5 E5 F♯5 G5 N.C.
End Voc. Fig. 1
Trib - al war-ri-ors. We will nev-er die. ______
nev-er die. We will nev-er die. We will.)
P.M.
Faster ♩ = 88
Bkgd. Voc.: w/ Voc. Fig. 1 (1 3/4 times)
F♯5 G5 A5 E5 F♯5 G5 A5 E5
We will nev-er die. ______ Trib - al war-ri-ors. ______
Rhy. Fig. 3
End Rhy. Fig. 3

Gtr. 1: w/ Rhy. Fig. 3 (3 times)
F#5 G5 A5 E5 F#5 G5 A5 E5 F#5 G5 A5 E5
We will nev-er die.
Trib - al war-ri - ors.
We will nev-er die.
F#5 G5 A5 E5 F#5 G5 A5 E5 F#5 G5 A5 E5
We will nev-er die.
We will nev-er die.
(...nev-er die.)
We will nev-er die.
Interlude
Slower ♩ = 78
F#5
N.C.
D5 E5 D5 E5
I wan-na know.
Gtr. 1
P.S.
Chorus
Gtr. 1: w/ Rhy. Fig. 1
F#5 G5 E5
1., 2., 3.
D5 A5 E5
Where do you stand in this bat-tle cry, trib-al sol-dier?
Rep-re-sent! I and I Jah Jah war-ri-ors.
4.
D5 E5 D5 E5
Rep-re-sent! I and I.
Outro
Gtr. 3: w/ Rhy. Fig. 2 (4 1/2 times)
F#5 G5 F#5 F#9(no3rd) F#m7 F#7(no3rd) F#9(no3rd) F#m7
Gtr. 1
1/2
* String noise from left hand movement.
Gtr. 1 tacet
F#7(no3rd) F#9(no3rd) F#m7 F#7(no3rd) F#9(no3rd) F#m7 F#7(no3rd)
Begin fade
Fade out
** Bass & drums segue (3/4 time, ♩ = 140) approximately 12 meas.

Freestyle

Words and Music by Sonny, Marcos, Traa and Wuv

Tune down 1 step:
(low to high) D–G–C–F–A–D

Intro
Slowly ♩ = 68

* Em(add9)   Caddb5

Gtr. 1 (clean) (backwards sound effects)
w/ delay
let ring throughout

* Chord symbols reflect basic harmony.
** Set for eighth-note regeneration with one repeat.

Verse
Moderately ♩ = 91
2nd time, Gtr. 2 tacet

E5   D5   Dsus4   D

1. Kids coming up from the alleys, not like the valleys. South-town San Diego rats out here in Cali-
2. It's bad enough late bills keep stacking up. No one ever told me that it would cost this much. So

Rhy. Fig. 1   End Rhy. Fig. 1

Gtr. 1: w/ Rhy. Fig. 1 (5 times)

E5   D5   Dsus4   D

So Cal with the crew to show 'em how. You like me now, with the sound straight underground. Put-
buckle up and come along for the ride. Catchin' the vibe and stayin' true to my tribe. I

E5   D5   Dsus4   D

tin' me down, lift up this jewel that I have found, and pass it around, flowing against the crowd. The
got mad love for the ones that still around. Knew you'd be down from the get-go here and now. You

E5   D5   Dsus4   D

hip-hop hard knox rhym'n soon as the tune drops. Negative small talks, homie start kickin' rocks.
make me proud from the diapers to the grave. No masquerade, stayed the same like in the day.

Copyright © 1999 by Souljah Music and Famous Music Corporation
International Copyright Secured   All Rights Reserved

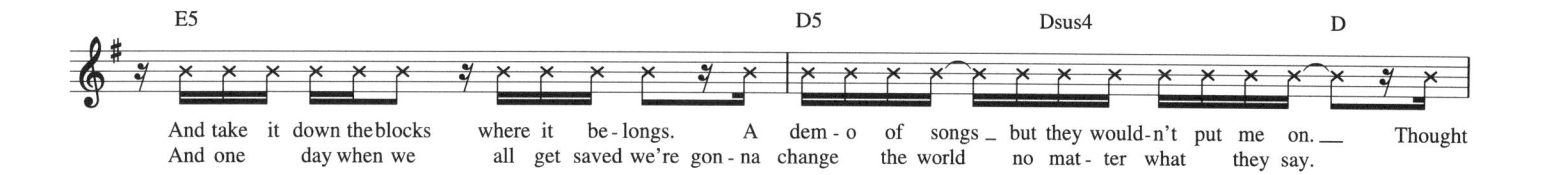

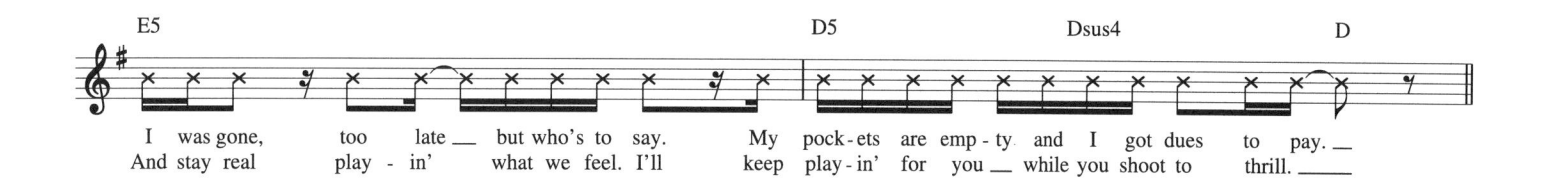

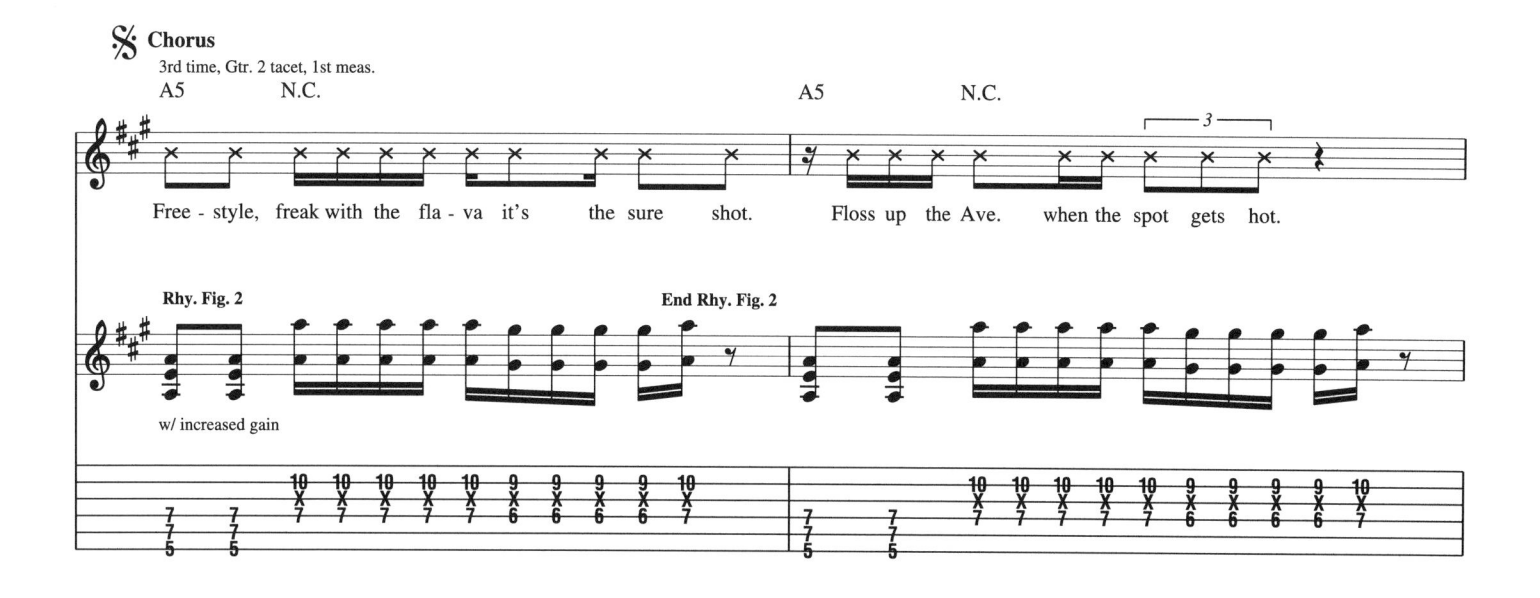

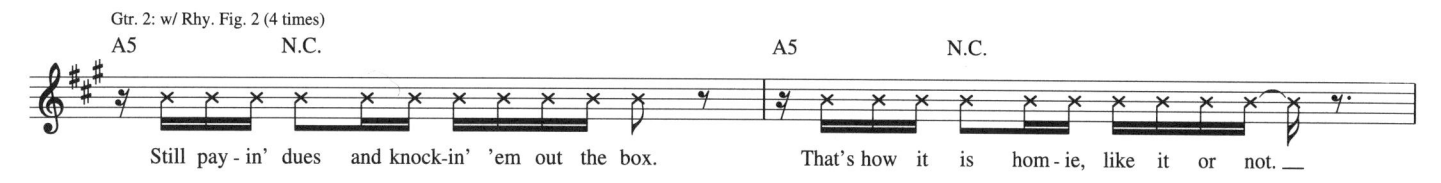

And take it down the blocks where it belongs. A demo of songs but they wouldn't put me on. Thought
And one day when we all get saved we're gonna change the world no matter what they say.

I was gone, too late but who's to say. My pockets are empty and I got dues to pay.
And stay real playin' what we feel. I'll keep playin' for you while you shoot to thrill.

Pre-chorus

Tic-toc you don't stop. To the tic-toc you don't quit, hit it.

Gtr. 2 (dist.)
Riff A ... End Riff A

*Doubled throughout

𝄋ᛋ Chorus
3rd time, Gtr. 2 tacet, 1st meas.

Freestyle, freak with the flava it's the sure shot. Floss up the Ave. when the spot gets hot.

Rhy. Fig. 2 ... End Rhy. Fig. 2
w/ increased gain

Gtr. 2: w/ Rhy. Fig. 2 (4 times)

Still payin' dues and knockin' 'em out the box. That's how it is homie, like it or not.

A5 N.C. A5 N.C.
Free - style, freak with the fla - va it's the sure shot. Floss up the Ave. when the spot gets hot.
A5 N.C. 1. A5 N.C.
Still pay-in' dues and knock-in' 'em out the box. That's how it is hom-ie, like it or not.
Gtr. 2
2. A5 N.C.
That's how it is hom-ie, like it or not.
Bridge
A5 E5 C5 E5 C5
It's been a long time. It's been a
Rhy. Fig. 3
End Rhy. Fig. 3
1st time, Gtr. 2: w/ Rhy. Fig. 3 (7 times)
2nd time, Gtr. 2: w/ Rhy. Fig. 3 (6 times)
A5 E5 C5 E5 C5 A5 E5 C5 E5 C5 A5 E5 C5 E5 C5
long time. It's been a long time. It's been a long time. It's
A5 E5 C5 E5 C5 A5 E5 C5 E5 C5
been a long time, been a long time com-in'. Been a long time, been a long time com-in'.

To Coda

| A5 | E5 | C5 | E5 C5 | A5 | E5 | C5 | E5 C5 |

Been a long time, been a long time com-in'. Been a long time, been a long time com-in'.

Verse
Gtr. 1: w/ Rhy. Fig. 1 (4 times)

| E5 | D5 | Dsus4 | D |

3. Hat-ed by man-y and loved by less, hold the thresh, res-ur-rec-ted here in the West.

| E5 | D5 | Dsus4 | D |

Clench the fist; dis-miss the ster-e-o-type myth. Loose lips sink ships, then plead the fifth.

| E5 | D5 | Dsus4 | D |

You hat-ed this, no rea-son you hat-ed this. If you on-ly knew, you'd be the first one to en-list.

| E5 | D5 | Dsus4 | D |

We come in love 'cause it's just how we does. Fit the frame, stay-in' the same as it ev-er was.

Pre-chorus
Gtr. 2: w/ Riff A (2 times)

| E5 |

Tic - toc you don't stop. To the tic - toc you don't quit. And to the

D.S. al Coda
(take 2nd ending)

Tic - toc you don't stop. To the tic - toc you don't quit, hit it.

⊕ Coda

| A5 | E5 | C5 | E5 C5 |

Been a long time been a long time com-in'.

(backwards sound effects)

Gtr. 2

rit.

* Approximately 8 seconds.

Follow Me

Words and Music by Sonny, Marcos, Traa and Wuv

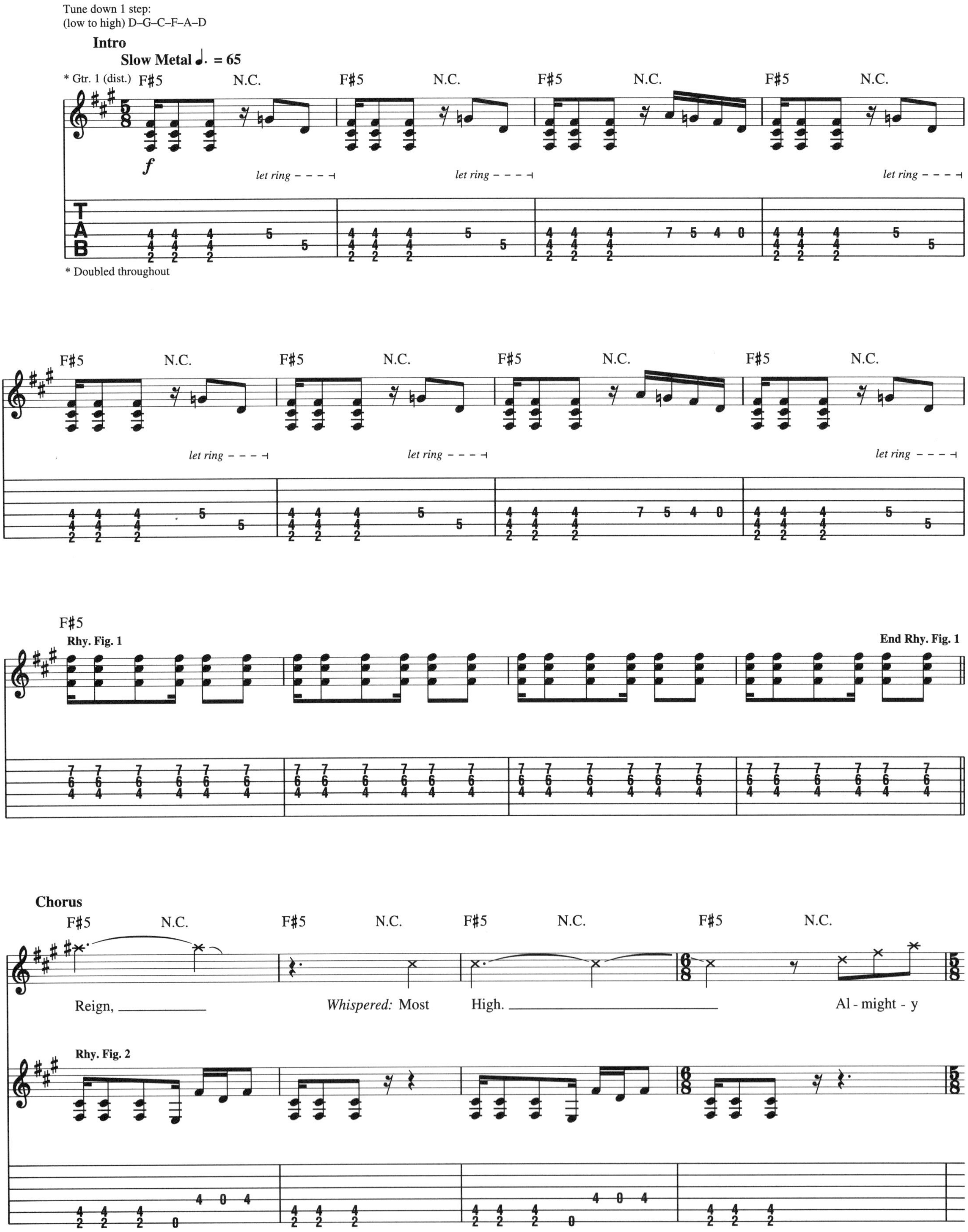

F#5 N.C. F#5 N.C. F#5 N.C. F#5 N.C.
reign, Whispered: Most High. Al-might-y
F#5 N.C. F#5 N.C. F#5 N.C. F#5 N.C.
I, Whispered: Most High. Al-might-y
F#5 N.C. F#5 N.C. F#5 N.C. F#5 N.C.
I, Whispered: Most High.
End Rhy. Fig. 2
F#5
Oo.
fdbk.
fdbk.

Verse

1. What good is it for a man to gain the whole world yet, yet lose or forfeit his very self? He must deny himself and take up his cross daily and follow me, follow me. If anyone is ashamed of me and my words, then I will be ashamed of them.

2. I tell you the truth. Some of you who are standing here will not taste death before they see Jah. Creation come with his power, power, power. What can a man give in exchange for his own soul he cannot save.

Pre-Chorus

When the time comes, in his Glory,

Chorus
Gtr. 1: w/ Rhy. Fig. 2
N.C.
F#5 N.C.
we will rise.
Reign,
Whispered: Most High.
Al-might-y
End Rhy. Fig. 4
reign,
Whispered: Most High.
Al-might-y I,
Whispered: Most High.
1st time, D.S. al Coda 1
2nd time, To Coda 2
Al-might-y I,
Whispered: Most High.
Coda 1
Interlude
Gtr. 1: w/ Rhy. Fig. 4 (last meas.)
Gtr. 1: w/ Rhy. Fig. 1 (2 1/2 times)
D.S.S. al Coda 2
we will rise.
(We will rise.)
Coda 2
Outro
Gtr. 1: w/ Rhy. Fig. 4
When the time comes in his Glo-ry,
we will rise.
Gtr. 1
1/4
P.S.

Outkast

Words and Music by Sonny, Marcos, Traa and Wuv

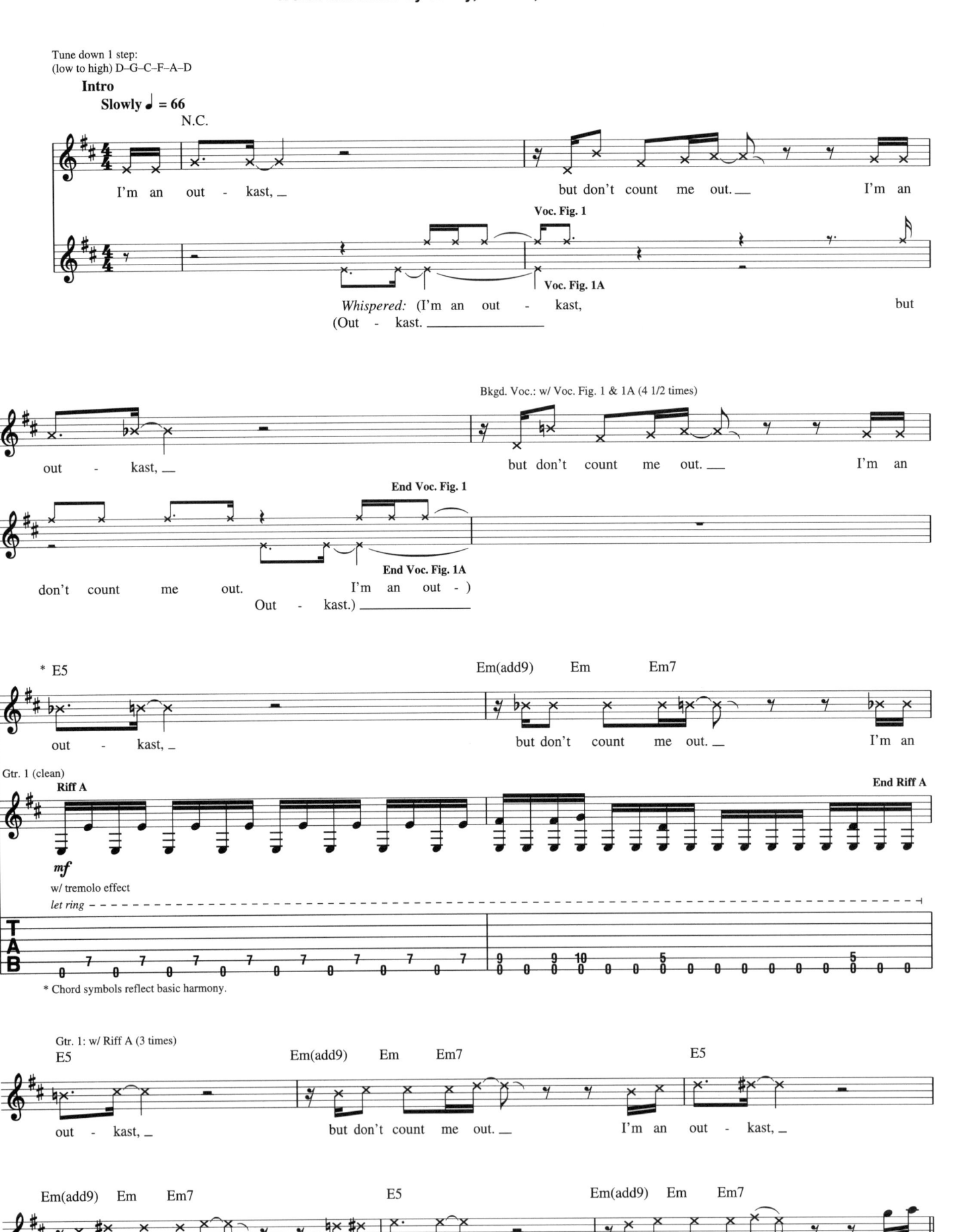

Tune down 1 step:
(low to high) D–G–C–F–A–D

Intro
Slowly ♩ = 66
N.C.

I'm an out - kast, _____ but don't count me out. _____ I'm an

Whispered: (I'm an out - kast, but
(Out - kast. _____

out - kast, _____ but don't count me out. _____ I'm an

Bkgd. Voc.: w/ Voc. Fig. 1 & 1A (4 1/2 times)

don't count me out. I'm an out -)
Out - kast.) _____

* E5   Em(add9)   Em   Em7

out - kast, _____ but don't count me out. _____ I'm an

Gtr. 1 (clean)
Riff A   **End Riff A**

mf
w/ tremolo effect
let ring - - - - - - - - - - - - - - - - - -

* Chord symbols reflect basic harmony.

Gtr. 1: w/ Riff A (3 times)
E5   Em(add9)   Em   Em7   E5

out - kast, _____ but don't count me out. _____ I'm an out - kast, _____

Em(add9)   Em   Em7   E5   Em(add9)   Em   Em7

but don't count me out. _____ I'm an out - kast, _____ but don't count me out. _____ I'm an

Copyright © 1999 by Souljah Music and Famous Music Corporation
International Copyright Secured   All Rights Reserved

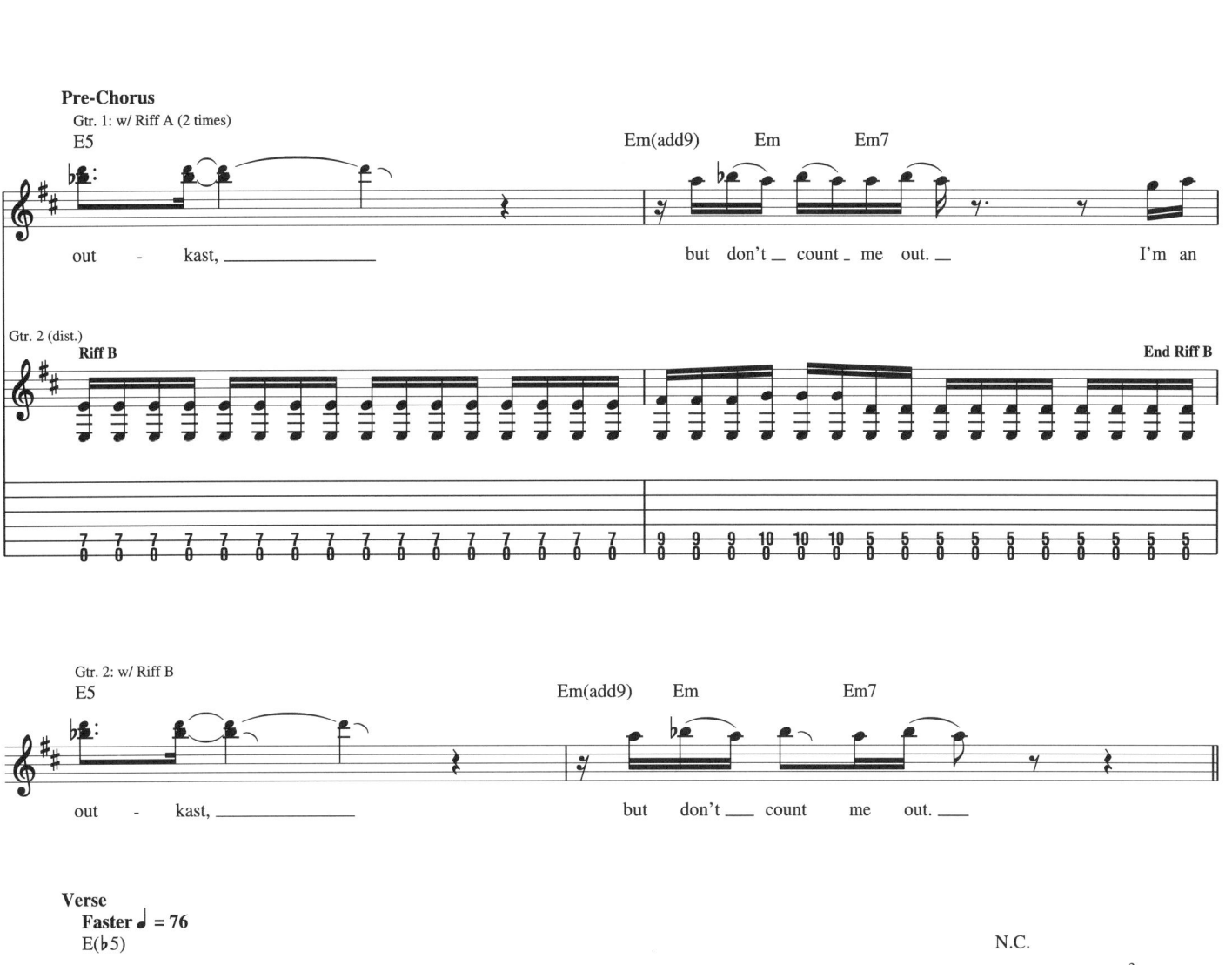

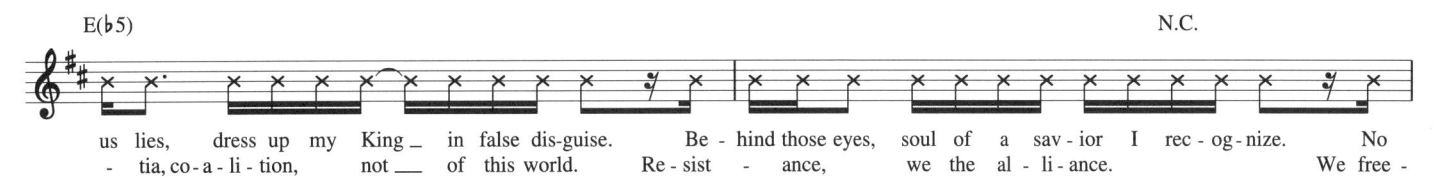

Pre-Chorus

out-kast, but don't count me out. I'm an

out-kast, but don't count me out.

Verse
Faster ♩ = 76

1. Un-der-ground dwell-az, roam-ing be-neath the cel-lars. Failed us with this sys-tem, ain't liv-ing how they tell us. Hide-
2. Dis-graced man, sur-vi-vors of the waste-land, look-ing for a home of his own. With no place

a-way place, it's safe, they raise a na-tion of hate, e-rase a man for his faith. They feed
to run and no place to hide, well it's time for you to stand on your own. Mi-li-

us lies, dress up my King in false dis-guise. Be-hind those eyes, soul of a sav-ior I rec-og-nize. No
-tia, co-a-li-tion, not of this world. Re-sist-ance, we the al-li-ance. We free-

65

com-pro-mise, while the whole world becomes cor-rupt. To-night we break the sur-face for lives, we com-ing up.
dom fight-ers, it's hon-or we de-fend. We fol-low truth and nev-er your trends.

Chorus

Broth-er take my hand. Let's sep-a-rate our-selves.

Leave be-hind this place. Don't ev-er look back.

Broth-er take my hand. Let's sep-a-rate our-selves.
(Hey.)

Rhy. Fill 1
Gtr. 2

1.
E5 G5 F#5 G5 F#5 E5 F5 E5 G5 F#5 G5 N.C.
And leave be - hind this place. Don't ev - er look back.
P.M.
2.
E5 G5 F#5 G5 F#5 E5 F5
Don't ev - er look back.
P.M.
Bridge
Slower ♩ = 66
Gtr. 2 tacet
Em
Voc. Fig. 3
Out - kast,
(Out - kast.)
* Gtr. 3 (clean)
mf
w/ envelope filter
* Two gtrs. arr. for one.
Bkgd. Voc.: w/ Voc. Fig. 3 (4 times)
don't ev - er count me out. I'm an out - kast,
End Voc. Fig. 3
1/2
1
w/ backwards effect
don't ev - er count me out. I'm an out - kast,
1
w/ pick & finger

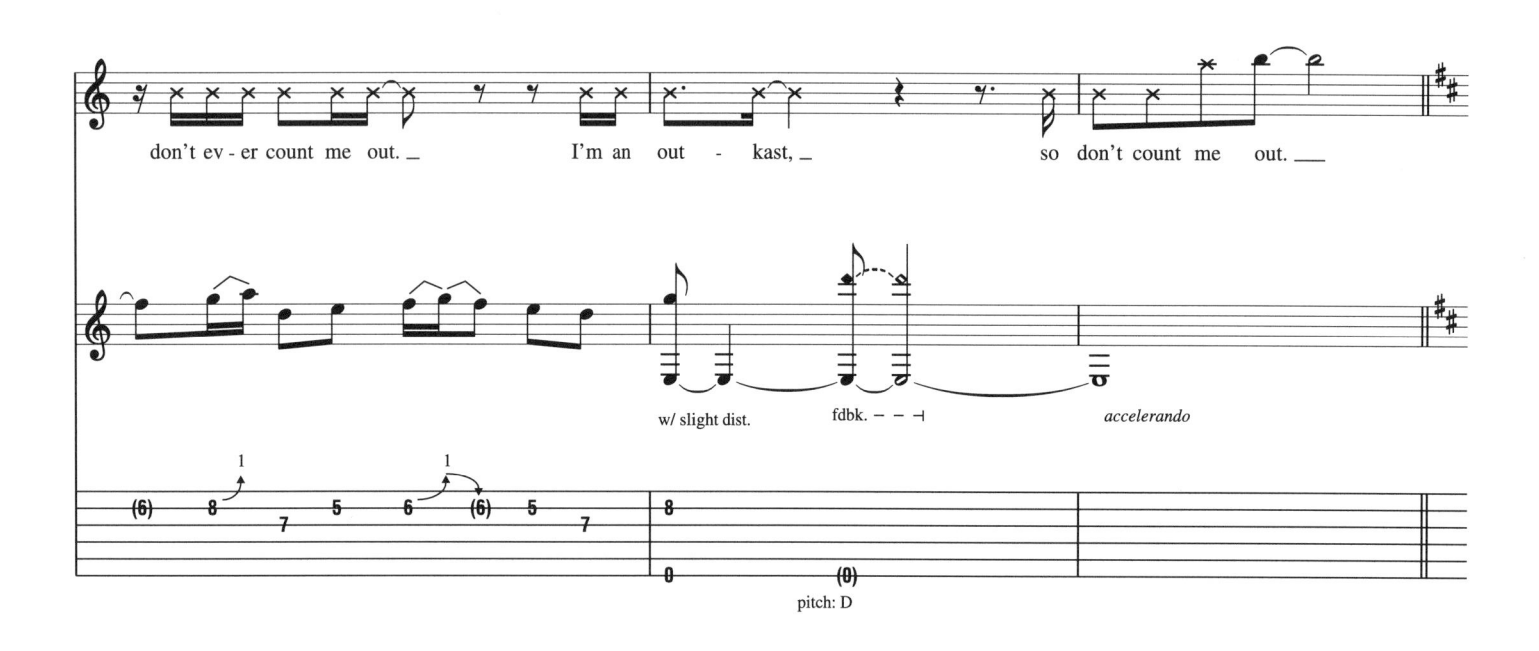

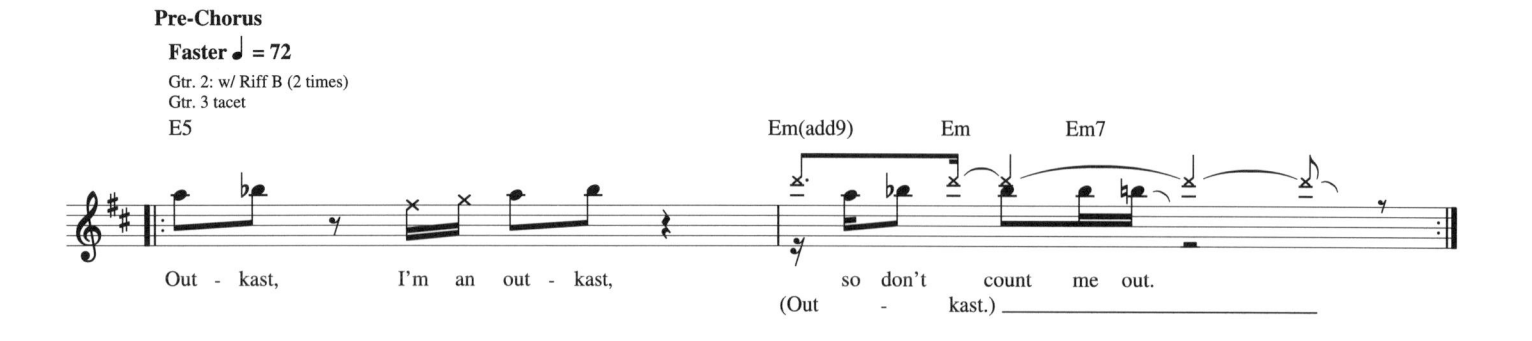

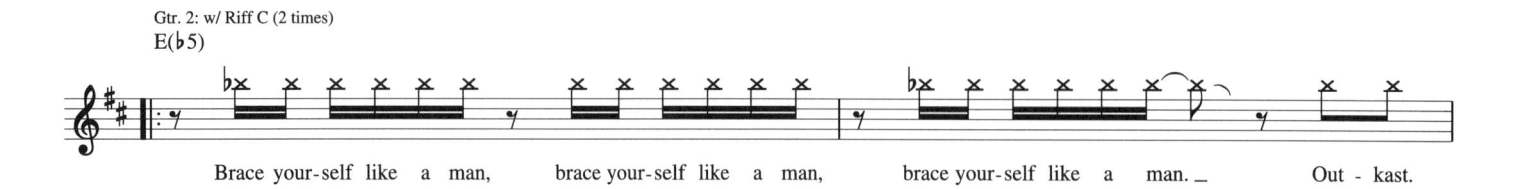

don't ev-er count me out. I'm an out-kast,

don't ev-er count me out. I'm an out-kast, so don't count me out.

w/ slight dist. fdbk. accelerando

pitch: D

Pre-Chorus
Faster ♩ = 72
Gtr. 2: w/ Riff B (2 times)
Gtr. 3 tacet

E5   Em(add9)   Em   Em7

Out-kast, I'm an out-kast, so don't count me out.
(Out - kast.)

Outro
Gtr. 2: w/ Riff C (2 times)
E(♭5)

Brace your-self like a man, brace your-self like a man, brace your-self like a man. Out-kast.

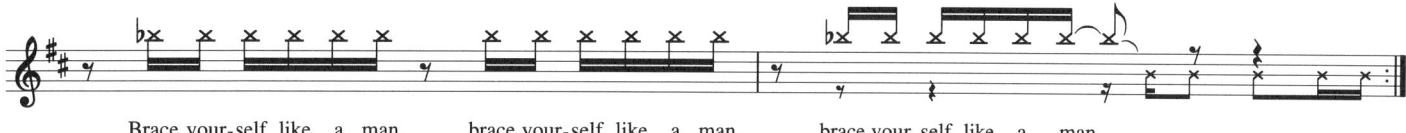

Brace your-self like a man, brace your-self like a man, brace your-self like a man. (So don't count me out.)

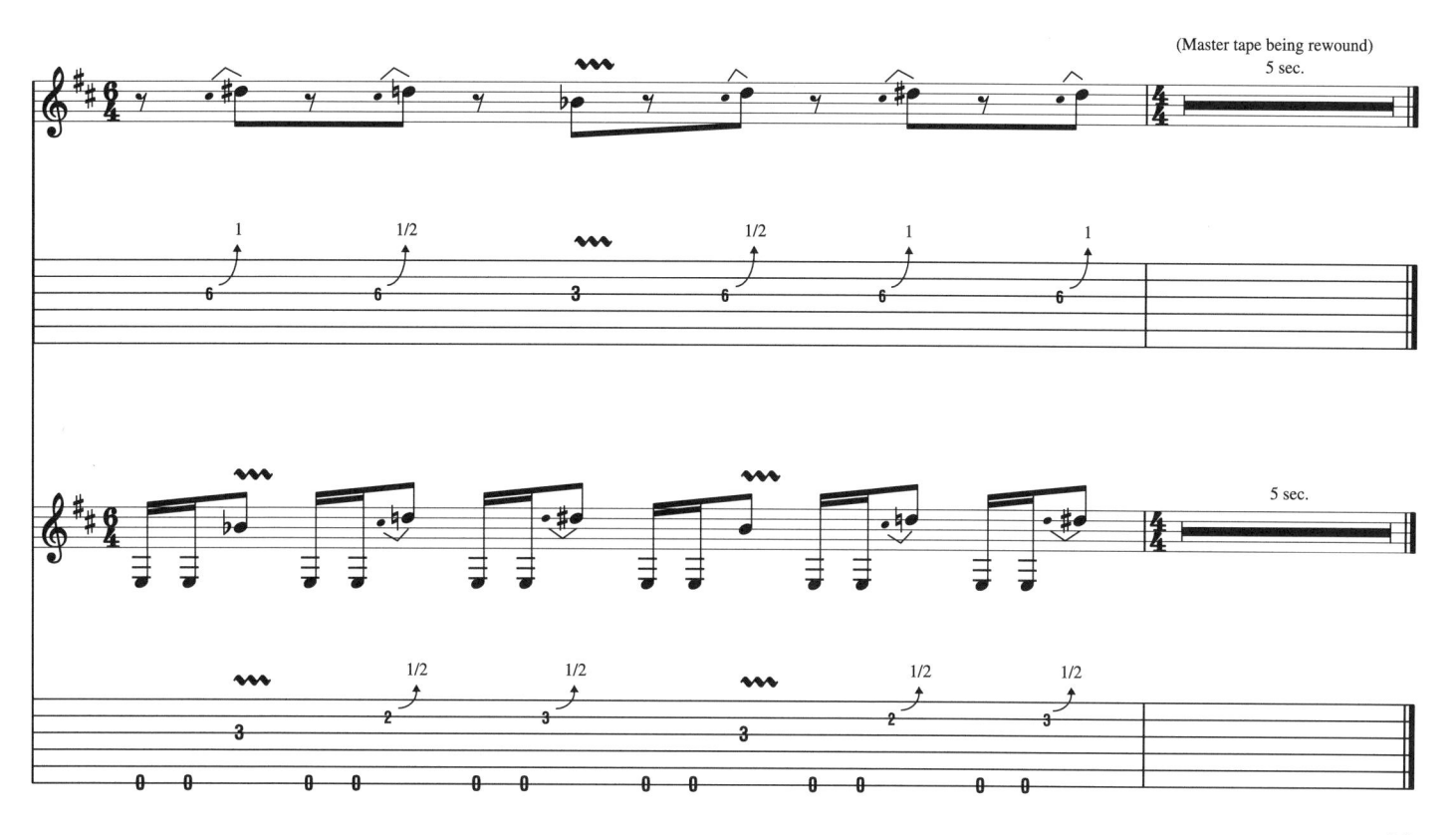

Faster ♩ = 76

E(♭5)

Gtr. 4 (dist.)

mf

Gtr. 2

(Master tape being rewound)
5 sec.

5 sec.

Tambura

Words and Music by Sonny, Marcos, Traa and Wuv

Tune down 1 step:
(low to high) D–G–C–F–A–D

*Chord symbols reflect basic harmony.

70

Coda 1
D
Em9
Dadd 4/9
Em9
Gtr. 2
Gtr. 1
Gtr. 3 (clean)
mp
w/ chorus & delay
mf
mp
Dadd 4/9
Em
Riff B
Harm.
mf

72

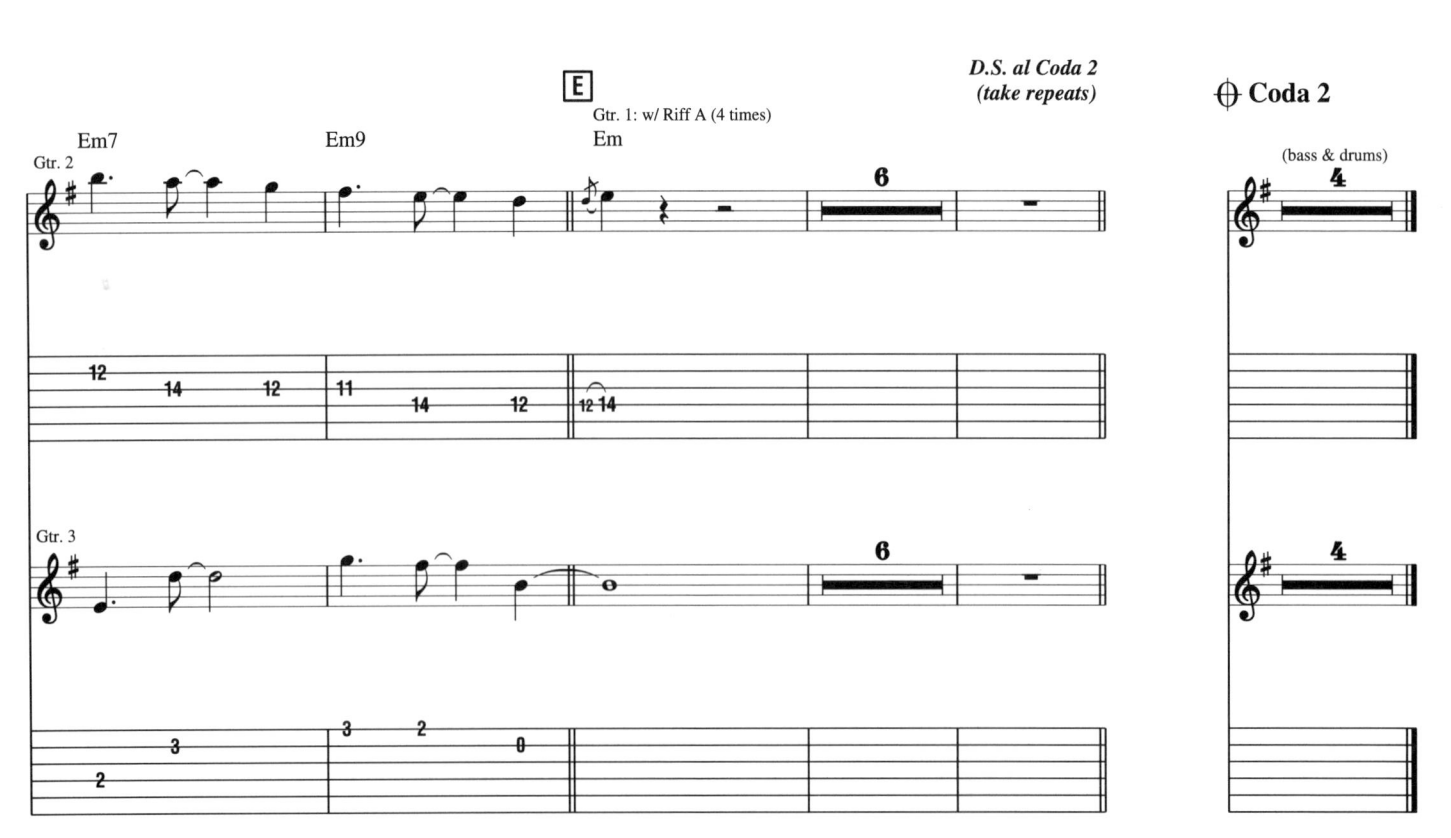